The Doctor and the Saint

The Doctor and the Saint

ARUNDHATI ROY

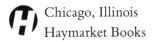

Chicago, Illinois
Haymarket Books

First published as the introduction to Ambedkar, *Anihilation of Caste: The Annotated Critical Edition*, in 2014 by Navayana Publishing Pvt Ltd.

Published in 2017 by
Haymarket Books
P.O. Box 180165
Chicago, IL 60618
773-583-7884
www.haymarketbooks.org
info@haymarketbooks.org

ISBN: 978-1-60846-797-6

Trade distribution:
In the US, Consortium Book Sales, www.cbsd.com
In Canada, Publishers Group Canada, www.pgcbooks.ca
In the UK, Turnaround Publisher Services, www.turnaround-uk.com
All other countries, Ingram Publisher Services International, ips_intlsales@ingramcontent.com

This book was published with the generous support of Lannan Foundation and Wallace Action Fund.

Printed in the United States.

Cover design by Abby Weintraub.

Library of Congress Cataloging-in-Publication data is available.

Entered into digital printing October 2018.

Contents

Preface

The Doctor and the Saint was originally written as an introduction for an annotated edition of Dr B.R. Ambedkar's iconic 1936 text, *Annihilation of Caste*, first published by Navayana in India, in 2014, and then by Verso Books in the United States and United Kingdom.

Annihilation of Caste is the text of a speech that Dr Ambedkar, one of India's greatest intellectuals, wrote but never delivered. Jat-Pat-Todak Mandal, the Hindu reformist organization that had invited him to address its members, all of them "upper-caste" Hindus, disinvited him after they read an advance copy of the text and realised that it was a frontal assault on Hinduism itself. Ambedkar went on to publish *Annihilation of Caste* as a pamphlet, which has since then been published mostly by small Dalit publishing houses, distributed in informal networks, and has, to date, sold millions of copies. From all accounts, B.R. Ambedkar is far and away the best-selling and most beloved author in India.

Soon after *Annihilation of Caste* was published, none other than Mohandas Gandhi, the most well-known Indian in the world, took issue with it. There followed a great public debate between the two men on this, perhaps the most vital issue in India then as well as now.

Despite this, and for reasons that will be obvious to anyone who reads it, *Annihilation of Caste* is not a text that is included in school or university syllabi. It is not available in bookshops. Nor has it been annotated with the scholarship and attention that it deserves. In other words, the people whom Ambedkar meant to address—in particular the 'moderate', reformist, Hindu 'upper castes' (although Ambedkar believed that 'moderate' and 'Hindu' are a contradiction in terms)—have managed to keep a kind of publishing and distribution 'segregation' in place, which helps, of course, to keep the very shameful practice of caste, India's own form of social apartheid, off the international radar.

The Doctor and the Saint looks at the practice of caste in India, through the prism of the present as well as the past. In seeking to give context to Gandhi's position on caste in his debate with Ambedkar I followed his story all the way back to his 'political awakening' in South Africa, which is now the stuff of legend and folklore. I will confess to being disturbed and taken aback at the scale and dishonesty of the mythology and falsehood that have obscured the facts of that story. Not by Gandhi as much as by his myth-makers.

I have been faulted for paying an inordinate amount of attention to Gandhi in an introduction to what is essentially Ambedkar's work. I am guilty as charged. However, given the exalted, almost divine status that Gandhi occupies in the imagination of the modern world, in particular the Western world, I felt that unless his hugely influential and, to my mind, inexcusable position on caste and race was looked at carefully, Ambedkar's rage would not be fully understood. And the Project of Unseeing, the erasure of cruel, institutionalised social injustice at the heart of the country that likes to be known as the world's greatest democracy, will continue smoothly and without a hitch.

For research in telling this story, I relied for the most part on Ambedkar's and Gandhi's own (copious) writings.

Arundhati Roy
January 2017

The Doctor and the Saint

The Doctor and the Saint

Annihilation of Caste is the nearly eighty-year-old text of a speech that was never delivered. When I first read it I felt as though somebody had walked into a dim room and opened the windows. Reading Dr Bhimrao Ramji Ambedkar bridges the gap between what most Indians are schooled to believe in and the reality we experience every day of our lives.

My father was a Hindu, a Brahmo. I never met him until I was an adult. I grew up with my mother in a Syrian Christian family in Ayemenem, a small village in communist-ruled Kerala. And yet all around me were the fissures and cracks of caste. Ayemenem had its own separate 'Paraiyan' church where 'Paraiyan' priests preached to an 'Untouchable' congregation. Caste was implied in people's names, in the way people referred to each other, in the work they did, in the clothes they wore, in the marriages that were arranged, in the language they spoke. Even so, I never encountered the notion of caste in a single school textbook. Reading Ambedkar alerted me to a gaping hole in our pedagogical universe. Reading him also made it clear why that hole exists and why it will continue to exist until Indian society undergoes radical, revolutionary change.

Revolutions can begin, and often have begun, with reading.

If you have heard of Malala Yousafzai but not of Surekha Bhotmange, then do read Ambedkar.

Malala was only fifteen but had already committed several

crimes. She was a girl, she lived in the Swat Valley in Pakistan, she was a BBC blogger, she was in a *New York Times* video, and she went to school. Malala wanted to be a doctor; her father wanted her to be a politician. She was a brave child. She (and her father) didn't take heed when the Taliban declared that schools were not meant for girls and threatened to kill her if she did not stop speaking out against them. On 9 October 2012, a gunman took her off her school bus and put a bullet through her head. Malala was flown to England, where, after receiving the best possible medical care, she survived. It was a miracle.

The US President and the Secretary of State sent messages of support and solidarity. Madonna dedicated a song to her. Angelina Jolie wrote an article about her. Malala was nominated for the Nobel Peace Prize; she was on the cover of *Time*. Within days of the attempted assassination, Gordon Brown, former British Prime Minister and the UN Special Envoy for Global Education, launched an 'I am Malala' petition that called on the Government of Pakistan to deliver education to every girl child. The US drone strikes in Pakistan continue with their feminist mission to 'take out' misogynist, Islamist terrorists.

Surekha Bhotmange was forty years old and had committed several crimes too. She was a woman—an 'Untouchable', Dalit woman—who lived in India, and she wasn't dirt poor. She was more educated than her husband, so she functioned as the head of her family. Dr Ambedkar was her hero. Like him, her family had renounced Hinduism and converted to Buddhism. Surekha's children were educated. Her two sons Sudhir and Roshan had been to college. Her daughter Priyanka was seventeen and finishing high school. Surekha and her husband had bought a little plot of land in the village of Khairlanji in the state of Maharashtra. It was surrounded by farms belonging to castes that considered themselves superior to the Mahar caste that Surekha belonged to. Because she was Dalit and had no right to aspire to

a good life, the village panchayat did not permit her to get an
electricity connection, or turn her thatched mud hut into a brick
house. The villagers would not allow her family to irrigate their
fields with water from the canal, or draw water from the public
well. They tried to build a public road through her land, and
when she protested, they drove their bullock carts through her
fields. They let their cattle loose to feed on her standing crop.

Still Surekha did not back down. She complained to the police,
who paid no attention to her. Over the months, the tension in
the village built to fever pitch. As a warning to her, the villagers
attacked a relative of hers and left him for dead. She filed another
police complaint. This time, the police made some arrests, but
the accused were released on bail almost immediately. At about
six in the evening of the day they were released (29 September
2006), about seventy incensed villagers, men and women, arrived
in tractors and surrounded the Bhotmanges' house. Her husband
Bhaiyalal, who was out in the fields, heard the noise and ran home.
He hid behind a bush and watched the mob attack his family. He
ran to Dusala, the nearest town, and through a relative managed
to call the police. (You need contacts to get the police to even
pick up the phone.) They never came. The mob dragged Surekha,
Priyanka and the two boys, one of them partially blind, out of
the house. The boys were ordered to rape their mother and sister;
when they refused, their genitals were mutilated, and eventually
they were lynched. Surekha and Priyanka were gang-raped and
beaten to death. The four bodies were dumped in a nearby canal,
where they were found the next day.[1]

At first, the press reported it as a 'morality' murder,
suggesting that the villagers were upset because Surekha was
having an affair with a relative (the man who had previously
been assaulted). Mass protests by Dalit organisations eventually
prodded the legal system into taking cognisance of the crime.
Citizens' fact-finding committees reported how evidence had

been tampered with and fudged. When the lower court finally pronounced a judgement, it sentenced the main perpetrators to death but refused to invoke the Scheduled Castes and Scheduled Tribes Prevention of Atrocities Act—the judge held that the Khairlanji massacre was a crime spurred by a desire for 'revenge'. He said there was no evidence of rape and no caste angle to the killing.[2] For a judgement to weaken the legal framework in which it presents a crime, for which it then awards the death sentence, makes it easy for a higher court to eventually reduce, or even commute, the sentence. This is not uncommon practice in India.[3] For a court to sentence people to death, however heinous their crime, can hardly be called just. For a court to acknowledge that caste prejudice continues to be a horrific reality in India would have counted as a gesture towards justice. Instead, the judge simply airbrushed caste out of the picture.

Surekha Bhotmange and her children lived in a market-friendly democracy. So there were no 'I am Surekha' petitions from the United Nations to the Indian government, nor any fiats or messages of outrage from heads of state. Which was just as well, because we don't want daisy-cutters dropped on us just because we practise caste.[4]

"To the Untouchables," Ambedkar said, with the sort of nerve that present-day intellectuals in India find hard to summon, "Hinduism is a veritable chamber of horrors."[5]

For a writer to have to use terms like 'Untouchable', 'Scheduled Caste', 'Backward Class' and 'Other Backward Classes' to describe fellow human beings is like living in a chamber of horrors. Since Ambedkar used the word 'Untouchable' with a cold rage, and without flinching, so must I. Today 'Untouchable' has been substituted with the Marathi word 'Dalit' (Broken People), which is, in turn, used interchangeably with 'Scheduled Caste'. This, as the scholar Rupa Viswanath points out, is incorrect practice, because the term 'Dalit' includes Untouchables who have converted to other religions to escape the stigma of caste (like the Paraiyans in my village who had converted to Christianity), whereas 'Scheduled Caste' does not.[6] The official nomenclature of prejudice is a maze that can make everything read like a bigoted bureaucrat's file notings. To try and avoid this, I have, mostly, though not always, used the word 'Untouchable' when I write about the past, and 'Dalit' when I write about the present. When I write about Dalits who have converted to other religions, I specifically say Dalit Sikhs, Dalit Muslims or Dalit Christians.

Let me now return to Ambedkar's point about the chamber of horrors.

According to the National Crime Records Bureau, a crime is committed against a Dalit by a non-Dalit every sixteen minutes; every day, more than four Untouchable women are raped by Touchables; every week, thirteen Dalits are murdered and six Dalits are kidnapped. In 2012 alone, the year of *the* Delhi gang-rape and murder,[7] 1,574 Dalit women were raped (the rule of thumb is that only 10 per cent of rapes or other crimes against Dalits are ever reported), and 651 Dalits were murdered.[8] That's just the rape and butchery. Not the stripping and parading naked, the forced shit-eating (literally),[9] the seizing of land, the social boycotts, the restriction of access to drinking water. These statistics wouldn't include, say, Bant Singh of Punjab, a Mazhabi Dalit Sikh,[10] who in 2005 had both his arms and a leg cleaved off for daring to file a case against the men who gang-raped his daughter. There are no separate statistics for triple amputees.

"If the fundamental rights are opposed by the community, no Law, no Parliament, no Judiciary can guarantee them in the real sense of the word", said Ambedkar. "What is the use of fundamental rights to the Negro in America, to the Jews in Germany and to the Untouchables in India? As Burke said, there is no method found for punishing the multitude".[11]

Ask any village policeman in India what his job is and he'll probably tell you it is to 'keep the peace'. That is done, most of the time, by upholding the caste system. Dalit aspirations are a breach of peace.

Annihilation of Caste is a breach of peace.

▼

Other contemporary abominations like apartheid, racism, sexism, economic imperialism and religious fundamentalism have been politically and intellectually challenged at international forums. How is it that the practice of caste in India—one of the most brutal modes of hierarchical social organisation that human society has known—has managed to escape similar scrutiny and censure? Perhaps because it has come to be so fused with Hinduism, and by extension with so much that is seen to be kind and good—mysticism, spiritualism, non-violence, tolerance, vegetarianism, Gandhi, yoga, backpackers, the Beatles—that, at least to outsiders, it seems impossible to pry it loose and try to understand it.

To compound the problem, caste, unlike say apartheid, is not colour-coded, and therefore not easy to *see*. Also, unlike apartheid, the caste system has buoyant admirers in high places. They argue, quite openly, that caste is a social glue that binds as well as separates people and communities in interesting and, on the whole, positive ways. That it has given Indian society the strength and the flexibility to withstand the many challenges it has had to face.[12] The Indian establishment blanches at the idea that discrimination and violence on the basis of caste can be compared to racism or to apartheid. It came down heavily on Dalits who tried to raise caste as an issue at the 2001 World Conference against Racism in Durban, insisting that caste was an "internal matter". It showcased theses by well-known sociologists who argued at length that the practice of caste was not the same as racial discrimination, and that caste was not the same as race.[13] Ambedkar would have agreed with them. However, in the context of the Durban conference, the point Dalit activists were making was that though caste is not the same as race, casteism and racism are indeed comparable. Both are forms of discrimination that target people because of their descent.[14] In solidarity with that sentiment, on 15 January 2014 at a public meeting on Capitol Hill in Washington D.C. commemorating Martin Luther King, Jr's 85th birth anniversary, African Americans signed "The Declaration of Empathy", which called for "an end to the oppression of Dalits in India".[15]

In the current debates about identity and justice, growth and development, for many of the best-known Indian scholars, caste is at best a topic, a subheading, and, quite often, just a footnote. By force-fitting caste into reductive Marxist class analysis, the progressive and left-leaning Indian intelligentsia has made seeing caste even harder. This erasure, this Project of Unseeing, is sometimes a conscious political act, and sometimes comes from a place of such rarefied privilege that caste has not been stumbled upon, not even in the dark, and therefore it is presumed to have been eradicated, like smallpox.

▼

The origins of caste will continue to be debated by anthropologists for years to come, but its organising principles, based on a hierarchical, sliding scale of entitlements and duties, of purity and pollution, and the ways in which they were, and still are, policed and enforced, are not all that hard to understand. The top of the caste pyramid is considered pure and has plenty of entitlements. The bottom is considered polluted and has no entitlements but plenty of duties. The pollution–purity matrix is correlated to an elaborate system of caste-based, ancestral occupation. In "Castes in India", a paper he wrote for a Columbia University seminar in 1916, Ambedkar defined a caste as an endogamous unit, an "enclosed class". On another occasion, he described the system as an "ascending scale of reverence and a descending scale of contempt".[16]

What we call the caste system today is known in Hinduism's founding texts as *varnashrama dharma* or *chaturvarna*, the system of four varnas. The approximately four thousand endogamous castes and sub-castes (*jatis*) in Hindu society, each with its own specified hereditary occupation, are divided into four varnas—Brahmins (priests), Kshatriyas (soldiers), Vaishyas (traders) and Shudras (servants). Outside of these varnas are the *avarna* castes, the Ati-Shudras, subhumans, arranged in hierarchies of their own—the Untouchables, the Unseeables, the Unapproachables—whose presence, whose touch, whose very shadow is considered to be polluting by privileged-caste Hindus. In some communities, to prevent inbreeding, each endogamous caste is divided into exogamous *gotras*. Exogamy is then policed with as much ferocity as endogamy—with beheadings and lynchings that have the approval of the community elders.[17] Each region of India has lovingly perfected its own unique version of caste-based cruelty, based on an unwritten code that is much worse than the Jim Crow laws. In addition to being forced to live in segregated settlements, Untouchables were not allowed to use the public roads that privileged castes used, they were not allowed to drink from common wells, they were not allowed into Hindu temples, they were not allowed into privileged-caste schools, they were not permitted to cover their upper bodies, they were only allowed to wear certain kinds of clothes and certain kinds of jewellery. Some castes, like the Mahars, the caste to which Ambedkar belonged, had to tie brooms to their waists to sweep away their polluted footprints, others had to hang spittoons around their necks to collect their polluted saliva.

Men of the privileged castes had undisputed rights over the bodies of Untouchable women. Love is polluting. Rape is pure. In many parts of India, much of this continues to this day.[18]

What remains to be said about an imagination, human or divine, that has thought up a social arrangement such as this? As if the dharma of varnashrama were not enough, there is also the burden of karma. Those born into the subordinated castes are supposedly being punished for the bad deeds they have done in their past lives. In effect, they are living out a prison sentence. Acts of insubordination could lead to an enhanced sentence, which would mean another cycle of rebirth as an Untouchable or as a Shudra. So it's best to behave.

"There cannot be a more degrading system of social organisation than the caste system", said Ambedkar. "It is the system that deadens, paralyses and cripples the people from helpful activity".[19]

The most famous Indian in the world, Mohandas Karamchand Gandhi, disagreed. He believed that caste represented the genius of Indian society. At a speech at a missionary conference in Madras in 1916, he said:

> The vast organisation of caste answered not only the religious wants of the community, but it answered too its political needs. The villagers managed their internal affairs through the caste system, and through it they dealt with any oppression from the ruling power or powers. It is not possible to deny the organising capability of a nation that was capable of producing the caste system its wonderful power of organisation.[20]

In 1921, in his Gujarati journal *Navajivan* he wrote:

> I believe that if Hindu Society has been able to stand, it is because it is founded on the caste system… To destroy the caste system and adopt the Western European social system means that Hindus must give up the principle of hereditary occupation which is the soul of the caste system. Hereditary principle is an eternal principle.

To change it is to create disorder. I have no use for a Brahmin if I cannot call him a Brahmin for my life. It will be chaos if every day a Brahmin is changed into a Shudra and a Shudra is to be changed into a Brahmin.[21]

Though Gandhi was an admirer of the caste system, he believed that there should be no hierarchy between castes; that all castes should be considered equal, and that the avarna castes, the Ati-Shudras, should be brought into the varna system. Ambedkar's response to this was that "the outcaste is a bye-product of the caste system. There will be outcastes as long as there are castes. Nothing can emancipate the outcaste except the destruction of the caste system".[22]

It has been almost seventy years since the August 1947 transfer of power between the imperial British government and the Government of India. Is caste in the past? How does varnashrama dharma play out in our new 'democracy'?

▼

A lot has changed. India has had a Dalit President and even a Dalit Chief Justice. The rise of political parties dominated by Dalits and other subordinated castes is a remarkable, and in some ways a revolutionary, development. Even if the form it has taken is that a small but visible minority—the leadership—lives out the dreams of the vast majority, given our history, the aggressive assertion of Dalit pride in the political arena can only be a good thing. The complaints about corruption and callousness brought against parties like the Bahujan Samaj Party (BSP) apply to the older political parties on an even larger scale, but charges levelled against the BSP take on a shriller, more insulting tone because its leader is someone like Mayawati, four-term Chief Minister of Uttar Pradesh—a Dalit, a single woman, and unapologetic about being both. Whatever the BSP's failings may be, its contribution towards building Dalit dignity is an immense political task that ought never to be minimised. The worry is that even as subordinated castes are becoming a force to reckon with in parliamentary democracy, democracy itself is being undermined in serious and structural ways.

After the fall of the Soviet Union, India, which was once at the forefront of the Non-Aligned Movement, repositioned itself as a 'natural ally' of the United States and Israel. In the 1990s, the Indian government embarked on a process of dramatic economic reforms, opening up a previously protected market to global capital, with natural resources, essential services and national infrastructure that had been developed over fifty years with public money now turned over to private corporations. Twenty years later, despite a spectacular GDP growth rate (which has recently slowed down), the new economic policies have led to the concentration of wealth in fewer and fewer hands. Today, India's one hundred richest people own assets equivalent to one-fourth of its celebrated GDP.[23] In a nation of 1.2 billion, more than 800 million people live on less than Rs 20 a day.[24] Giant corporations virtually own and run the country. Politicians and political parties have begun to function as subsidiary holdings of big business.

How has this affected traditional caste networks? Some argue that caste has insulated Indian society and prevented it from fragmenting and atomising like Western society did after the industrial revolution.[25] Others argue the opposite; they say that the unprecedented levels of urbanisation and the creation of a new work environment have shaken up the old order and rendered caste hierarchies irrelevant if not obsolete. Both claims deserve serious attention. Pardon the somewhat unliterary interlude that follows, but generalisations cannot replace facts.

A recent list of dollar billionaires published by *Forbes* magazine features fifty-five Indians.[26] The figures, naturally, are based on revealed wealth. Even among these dollar billionaires the distribution of wealth is a steep pyramid in which the cumulative wealth of the top ten outstrips the forty-five below them. Seven out of those top ten are Vaishyas, all of them CEOs of major corporations with business interests all over the world. Between them they own and operate ports, mines, oilfields, gas fields, shipping companies, pharmaceutical companies, telephone networks, petrochemical plants, aluminium plants, cellphone networks, television channels, fresh food outlets, high schools, film production companies, stem cell storage systems, electricity supply networks and Special Economic Zones. They are: Mukesh Ambani (Reliance Industries Ltd), Lakshmi Mittal (Arcelor Mittal), Dilip Shanghvi (Sun Pharmaceuticals), the Ruia brothers (Ruia Group), K.M. Birla (Aditya Birla Group), Savitri Devi Jindal (O.P. Jindal Group), Gautam Adani (Adani Group) and Sunil Mittal (Bharti Airtel). Of the remaining forty-five, nineteen are Vaishyas too. The rest are for the most part Parsis, Bohras and Khattris (all mercantile castes) and Brahmins. There are no Dalits or Adivasis in this list.

Apart from big business, Banias (Vaishyas) continue to have a firm hold on small trade in cities and on traditional rural moneylending across the country, which has millions of impoverished peasants and Adivasis, including those who live deep in the forests of Central India, caught in a spiralling debt trap. The tribal-dominated states in India's North East—Arunachal Pradesh, Manipur, Mizoram, Tripura, Meghalaya, Nagaland and Assam—have, since 'independence', witnessed decades of insurgency, militarisation and bloodshed. Through all this, Marwari and Bania traders have settled there, kept a low profile, and consolidated their businesses. They now control almost all the economic activity in the region.

In the 1931 Census, which was the last to include caste as an aspect of the survey, Vaishyas accounted for 2.7 per cent of the population (while the Untouchables accounted for 12.5 per cent).[27] Given their access to better health care and more secure futures for their children, the figure for Vaishyas is likely to have decreased rather than increased. Either way, their economic clout in the new economy is extraordinary. In big business and small, in agriculture as well as industry, caste and capitalism have blended into a disquieting, uniquely Indian alloy. Cronyism is built into the caste system.

Vaishyas are only doing their divinely ordained duty. The *Arthashastra* (circa 350 BCE) says usury is the Vaishya's right. The *Manusmriti* (circa 150 CE) goes further and suggests a sliding scale of interest rates: 2 per cent per month for Brahmins, 3 per cent for Kshatriyas, 4 per cent for Vaishyas and 5 per cent for Shudras.[28] On an annual basis, the Brahmin was to pay 24 per cent interest and the Shudra and Dalit, 60 per cent. Even today, for moneylenders to charge a desperate farmer or landless labourer an annual interest of 60 per cent (or more) for a loan is quite normal. If they cannot pay in cash, they have to pay what is known as 'bodily interest', which means they are expected to toil for the moneylender from generation to generation to repay impossible debts. It goes without saying that according to the *Manusmriti* no one can be forced into the service of anyone belonging to a 'lower' caste.

Vaishyas control Indian business. What do the Brahmins— the *bhudevas* (gods on earth)—do? The 1931 Census puts their population at 6.4 per cent, but, like the Vaishyas and for similar reasons, that percentage too has probably declined. According to a survey by the Centre for the Study of Developing Societies (CSDS), from having a disproportionately high number of representatives in Parliament, Brahmins have seen their numbers drop dramatically.[29] Does this mean Brahmins have become less influential?

According to Ambedkar, Brahmins, who were 3 per cent of the population in the Madras Presidency in 1948, held 37 per cent of the gazetted posts and 43 per cent of the non-gazetted posts in government jobs.[30] There is no longer a reliable way to keep track of these trends because after 1931 the Project of Unseeing set in. In the absence of information that ought to be available, we have to make do with what we can find. In a 1990 piece called "Brahmin Power", the writer Khushwant Singh said:

> Brahmins form no more than 3.5 per cent of the population of our country… today they hold as much as 70 per cent of government jobs. I presume the figure refers only to gazetted posts. In the senior echelons of the civil service from the rank of deputy secretaries upward, out of 500 there are 310 Brahmins, i.e. 63 per cent; of the 26 state chief secretaries, 19 are Brahmins; of the 27 Governors and Lt Governors, 13 are Brahmins; of the 16 Supreme Court Judges, 9 are Brahmins; of the 330 judges of High Courts, 166 are Brahmins; of 140 ambassadors, 58 are Brahmins; of the total 3,300 IAS officers, 2,376 are Brahmins. They do equally well in electoral posts; of the 508 Lok Sabha members, 190 were Brahmins; of 244 in the Rajya Sabha, 89 are Brahmins. These statistics clearly prove that this 3.5 per cent of Brahmin community of India holds between 36 per cent to 63 per cent of all the plum jobs available in the country. How this has come about I do not know. But I can scarcely believe that it is entirely due to the Brahmin's higher IQ.[31]

The statistics Khushwant Singh cites may be flawed, but are unlikely to be drastically flawed. They are a quarter of a century old now. Some new census-based information would help, but is unlikely to be forthcoming.

According to the CSDS study, 47 per cent of all Supreme Court Chief Justices between 1950 and 2000 were Brahmins. During the same period, 40 per cent of the Associate Justices in the High Courts and lower courts were Brahmin. The Backward Classes Commission, in a 2007 report, said that 37.17 per cent of the Indian bureaucracy was made up of Brahmins. Most of them occupied the top posts.

Brahmins have also traditionally dominated the media. Here too, what Ambedkar said in 1945 still has resonance:

The Untouchables have no Press. The Congress Press is closed to them and is determined not to give them the slightest publicity. They cannot have their own Press and for obvious reasons. No paper can survive without advertisement revenue. Advertisement revenue can come only from business and in India all business, both high and small, is attached to the Congress and will not favour any Non-Congress organisation. The staff of the Associated Press in India, which is the main news distributing agency in India, is entirely drawn from the Madras Brahmins—indeed the whole of the Press in India is in their hands—and they, for well-known reasons, are entirely pro-Congress and will not allow any news hostile to the Congress to get publicity. These are reasons beyond the control of the Untouchables.[32]

In 2006, the CSDS did a survey on the social profile of New Delhi's media elite. Of the 315 key decision-makers surveyed from thirty-seven Delhi-based Hindi and English publications and television channels, almost 90 per cent of the decision-makers in the English language print media and 79 per cent in television were found to be 'upper caste'. Of them, 49 per cent were Brahmins. Not one of the 315 was a Dalit or an Adivasi; only 4 per cent belonged to castes designated as Shudra, and 3 per cent were Muslim (who make up 13.4 per cent of the population).

That's the journalists and the 'media personalities'. Who owns the big media houses that they work for? Of the four most important English national dailies, three are owned by Vaishyas and one by a Brahmin family concern. The Times Group (Bennett, Coleman Company Ltd), the largest mass media company in India, whose holdings include *The Times of India* and the 24-hour news channel Times Now, is owned by the Jain family (Banias). The *Hindustan Times* is owned by the Bhartiyas, who are Marwari Banias; the *Indian Express* by the Goenkas, also Marwari Banias; *The Hindu* is owned by a Brahmin family concern; the *Dainik Jagran* Hindi daily, which is the largest selling newspaper in India with a circulation of fifty-five million, is owned by the Gupta family, Banias from Kanpur. *Dainik Bhaskar*, among the most influential Hindi dailies with a circulation of 17.5 million, is owned by Agarwals, Banias again. Reliance Industries Ltd (owned by Mukesh Ambani, a Gujarati Bania) has controlling shares in twenty-seven major national and regional TV channels. The Zee TV network, one of the largest national TV news and entertainment networks, is owned by Subhash Chandra, also a Bania. (In southern India, caste manifests itself somewhat differently. For example, the Eenadu Group—which owns newspapers, the largest film city in the world and a dozen TV channels, among other things—is headed by Ramoji Rao of the Kamma peasant caste of Andhra Pradesh, which bucks the trend of Brahmin–Bania ownership of Big Media. Another major media house, the Sun TV group, is owned by the Marans, who are designated as a 'backward' caste, but are politically powerful today.)

After independence, in an effort to right a historic wrong, the Indian government implemented a policy of reservation (positive discrimination) in universities and for jobs in state-run bodies for those who belong to Scheduled Castes and Scheduled Tribes.[33] Reservation is the only opportunity the Scheduled Castes have to break into the mainstream. (Of course, the policy does not apply to Dalits who have converted to other religions but continue to face discrimination.) To be eligible for the reservation policy, a Dalit needs to have completed high school. According to government data, 71.3 per cent of Scheduled Caste students drop out before they matriculate, which means that even for low-end government jobs, the reservation policy only applies to one in every four Dalits.[34] The minimum qualification for a white-collar job is a graduate degree. According to the 2001 Census, only 2.24 per cent of the Dalit population are graduates.[35] The policy of reservation, however minuscule the percentage of the Dalit population it applies to, has nevertheless given Dalits an opportunity to find their way into public services, to become doctors, scholars, writers, judges, policemen and officers of the civil services. Their numbers are small, but the fact that there is some Dalit representation in the echelons of power alters old social equations. It creates situations that were unimaginable even a few decades ago in which, say, a Brahmin clerk may have to serve under a Dalit civil servant.[36] Even this tiny opportunity that Dalits have won for themselves washes up against a wall of privileged-caste hostility.

The National Commission for Scheduled Castes and Scheduled Tribes, for example, reports that in Central Public Sector Enterprises, only 8.4 per cent of the A-Grade officers (pardon the horrible term) belong to the Scheduled Castes, when the figure should be 15 per cent.

The same report has some disturbing statistics about the representation of Dalits and Adivasis in India's judicial services: among Delhi's twenty High Court judges, not one belonged to the Scheduled Castes, and in all other judicial posts, the figure was 1.2 per cent; similar figures were reported from Rajasthan; Gujarat had no Dalit or Adivasi judges; in Tamil Nadu, with its legacy of social justice movements, only four out of thirty-eight High Court judges were Dalit; Kerala, with its Marxist legacy, had one Dalit High Court judge among twenty-five.[37] A study of the prison population would probably reveal an inverse ratio.

Former President K.R. Narayanan, a Dalit himself, was mocked by the judicial fraternity when he suggested that Scheduled Castes and Tribes, who according to the 2011 Census make up 25 per cent of India's 1.2 billion population, should find proportionate representation as judges in the Supreme Court. "Eligible persons from these categories are available and their under-representation or non-representation would not be justifiable", he said in 1999. "Any reservation in judiciary is a threat to its independence and the rule of law", was the response of a senior Supreme Court advocate. Another high-profile legal luminary said: "Job quotas are a vexed subject now. I believe the primacy of merit must be maintained".[38]

'Merit' is the weapon of choice for an Indian elite that has dominated a system by allegedly divine authorisation, and denied knowledge—of certain kinds—to the subordinated castes for thousands of years. Now that it is being challenged, there have been passionate privileged-caste protests against the policy of reservation in government jobs and student quotas in universities. The presumption is that 'merit' exists in an ahistorical social vacuum and that the advantages that come from privileged-caste social networking and the establishment's entrenched hostility towards the subordinated castes are not factors that deserve consideration. In truth, 'merit' has become a euphemism for nepotism.

In Jawaharlal Nehru University (JNU)—which is regarded as a bastion of progressive social scientists and historians—only 3.29 per cent of the faculty is Dalit and 1.44 per cent Adivasi,[39] while the quotas are meant to be 15 per cent and 7.5 per cent respectively. This, despite having supposedly implemented reservation for twenty-seven years. In 2010, when the subject was raised, some of its Professors Emeritus said that implementing the constitutionally mandated reservation policy would "prevent JNU from remaining one of the premier centres of excellence".[40] They argued that if reservation was implemented in faculty positions at JNU, "the well-to-do will move to foreign and private universities, and the disadvantaged will no longer be able to get world class education which JNU has been so proud to offer them so far".[41] B.N. Mallick, a professor of life sciences, was less shy: "Some castes are genetically malnourished and so very little can be achieved in raising them up; and if they are, it would be undoing excellence and merit."[42] Year after year, privileged-caste students have staged mass protests against reservation across India.

That's the news from the top. At the other end of New India, the Sachar Committee Report tells us that Dalits and Adivasis still remain at the bottom of the economic pyramid where they always were, below the Muslim community.[43] We know that Dalits and Adivasis make up the majority of the millions of people displaced by mines, dams and other major infrastructure projects. They are the pitifully low-paid farm workers and the contract labourers who work in the urban construction industry. Seventy per cent of Dalits are by and large landless. In states like Punjab, Bihar, Haryana and Kerala, the figure is as high as 90 per cent.[44]

There is one government department in which Dalits are over-represented by a factor of six. Almost 90 per cent of those designated as sweepers—who clean streets, who go down manholes and service the sewage system, who clean toilets and do menial jobs—and employed by the Government of India are Dalits.[45] (Even this sector is up for privatisation now, which means private companies will be able to subcontract jobs on a temporary basis to Dalits for less pay and with no guarantee of job security.)

While janitors' jobs in malls and in corporate offices with swanky toilets that do not involve 'manual scavenging' go to non-Dalits, there are (officially) 1.3 million people,[46] mostly women, who continue to earn their living by carrying baskets of human shit on their heads as they clean out traditional-style toilets that use no water. Though it is against the law, the Indian

Railways is one of the biggest employers of manual scavengers. Its 14,300 trains transport twenty-five million passengers across 65,000 kilometres every day. Their shit is funnelled straight onto the railway tracks through 172,000 open-discharge toilets. This shit, which must amount to several tonnes a day, is cleaned by hand, without gloves or any protective equipment, exclusively by Dalits.[47] While the Prohibition of Employment as Manual Scavengers and their Rehabilitation Bill, 2012, was cleared by the Cabinet and by the Rajya Sabha in September 2013, the Indian Railways has ignored it. With deepening poverty and the steady evaporation of government jobs, a section of Dalits has to fiercely guard its 'permanent' state employment as hereditary shit-cleaners against predatory interlopers.

A few Dalits have managed to overcome these odds. Their personal stories are extraordinary and inspirational. Some Dalit businessmen and women have come together to form their own institution, the Dalit Indian Chamber of Commerce and Industry (DICCI), which is praised and patronised by big business and given plenty of play on television and big media because it helps to give the impression that as long as you work hard, capitalism is intrinsically egalitarian.[48]

Time was when a caste Hindu crossing the oceans was said to have lost caste and become polluted. Now, the caste system is up for export. Wherever Hindus go, they take it with them. It exists among the brutalised Tamils in Sri Lanka; it exists among upwardly mobile Indian immigrants in the 'Free World', in Europe as well as in the United States. For about ten years, Dalit-led groups in the UK have been lobbying to have caste discrimination recognised by British law as a form of racial discrimination. Caste-Hindu lobbies have managed to scuttle it for the moment.[49]

Democracy hasn't eradicated caste. It has entrenched and modernised it. This is why it's time to read Ambedkar.

▼

Ambedkar was a prolific writer. Unfortunately his work, unlike the writings of Gandhi, Nehru or Vivekananda, does not shine out at you from the shelves of libraries and bookshops. Of his many volumes, *Annihilation of Caste* is his most radical text. It is not an argument directed at Hindu fundamentalists or extremists, but at those who considered themselves moderate, those whom Ambedkar called "the best of Hindus"—and some academics call "left-wing Hindus".[50] Ambedkar's point is that to believe in the Hindu shastras and to simultaneously think of oneself as liberal or moderate is a contradiction in terms. When the text of *Annihilation of Caste* was published, the man who is often called the 'Greatest of Hindus'—Mahatma Gandhi— responded to Ambedkar's provocation.

Their debate was not a new one. Both men were their generation's emissaries of a profound social, political and philosophical conflict that had begun long ago and has still by no means ended. Ambedkar, the Untouchable, was heir to the anticaste intellectual tradition that goes back to 200–100 BCE. The practice of caste, which is believed to have its genesis in the Purusha Sukta hymn[51] in the *Rig Veda* (1200–900 BCE), faced its first challenge only a thousand years later, when the Buddhists broke with caste by creating sanghas that admitted everybody, regardless of which caste they belonged to. Yet caste endured and evolved. In the mid-twelfth century, the Veerashaivas led by Basava challenged caste in South India, and were crushed. From the fourteenth century onwards, the beloved Bhakti poet-saints—Cokhamela, Ravidas, Kabir, Tukaram, Mira, Janabai— became, and still remain, the poets of the anticaste tradition. In the nineteenth and early twentieth centuries came Jotiba Phule and his Satyashodhak Samaj in western India; Pandita Ramabai, perhaps India's first feminist, a Marathi Brahmin who rejected Hinduism and converted to Christianity (and challenged that too); Swami Achhutanand Harihar, who led the Adi Hindu movement, started the Bharatiya Achhut Mahasabha (Parliament of Indian Untouchables), and edited *Achhut*, the first Dalit journal; Ayyankali and Sree Narayana Guru, who shook up the old order in Malabar and Travancore; the iconoclast Iyothee Thass and his Sakya Buddhists, who ridiculed Brahmin supremacy in the Tamil world. Among Ambedkar's contemporaries in the anticaste tradition were E.V. Ramasamy Naicker, known as 'Periyar' in the Madras Presidency, Jogendranath Mandal of Bengal, and Babu Mangoo Ram, who founded the Ad Dharm movement in the Punjab that rejected both Sikhism and Hinduism. These were Ambedkar's people.

Gandhi, a Vaishya, born into a Gujarati Bania family, was the latest in a long tradition of privileged-caste Hindu reformers and their organisations—Raja Ram Mohan Roy, who founded the Brahmo Samaj in 1828; Swami Dayananda Saraswati, who founded the Arya Samaj in 1875; Swami Vivekananda, who established the Ramakrishna Mission in 1897 and a host of other, more contemporary reformist organisations.[52]

Putting the Ambedkar–Gandhi debate into context for those unfamiliar with its history and its protagonists will require detours into their very different political trajectories. For this was by no means just a theoretical debate between two men who held different opinions. Each represented very separate interest groups, and their battle unfolded in the heart of India's national movement. What they said and did continues to have an immense bearing on contemporary politics. Their differences were (and remain) irreconcilable. Both are deeply loved and often deified by their followers. It pleases neither constituency to have the other's story told, though the two are inextricably linked. Ambedkar was Gandhi's most formidable adversary.

He challenged him not just politically or intellectually, but also morally. To have excised Ambedkar from Gandhi's story, which is the story we all grew up on, is a travesty. Equally, to ignore Gandhi while writing about Ambedkar is to do Ambedkar a disservice, because Gandhi loomed over Ambedkar's world in myriad and un-wonderful ways.

▼

The Indian national movement, as we know, had a stellar cast. It has even been the subject of a Hollywood blockbuster that won eight Oscars. In India, we have made a pastime of holding opinion polls and publishing books and magazines in which our constellation of founding fathers (mothers don't make the cut) are arranged and rearranged in various hierarchies and formations. Mahatma Gandhi does have his bitter critics, but he still tops the charts. For others to even get a look-in, the Father of the Nation has to be segregated, put into a separate category: Who, after Mahatma Gandhi, is the greatest Indian?[53]

Dr Ambedkar (who, incidentally, did not even have a walk-on part in Richard Attenborough's *Gandhi*, though the film was co-funded by the Indian government) almost always makes it into the final heat. He is chosen more for the part he played in drafting the Indian Constitution than for the politics and the passion that were at the core of his life and thinking. You definitely get the sense that his presence on the lists is the result of positive discrimination, a desire to be politically correct. The caveats continue to be murmured: 'opportunist' (because he served as Labour Member of the British Viceroy's Executive Council, 1942–46), 'British stooge' (because he accepted an invitation from the British government to the First Round Table Conference in 1930 when Congressmen were being imprisoned for breaking the salt laws), 'separatist' (because he wanted separate electorates for Untouchables), 'anti-national' (because he endorsed the Muslim League's case for Pakistan, and because he suggested that Jammu and Kashmir be trifurcated).[54]

Notwithstanding the name-calling, the fact, as we shall see, is that neither Ambedkar nor Gandhi allows us to pin easy labels on them that say 'pro-imperialist' or 'anti-imperialist'. Their conflict complicates and perhaps enriches our understanding of imperialism as well as the struggle against it.

History has been kind to Gandhi. He was deified by millions of people in his own lifetime. Gandhi's godliness has become a universal and, so it seems, an eternal phenomenon. It's not just that the metaphor has outstripped the man. It has entirely reinvented him. (Which is why a critique of Gandhi need not automatically be taken to be a critique of all Gandhians.) Gandhi has become all things to all people: Obama loves him and so does the Occupy movement. Anarchists love him and so does the Establishment. Narendra Modi loves him and so does Rahul Gandhi. The poor love him and so do the rich.

He is the Saint of the Status Quo.

Gandhi's life and his writing—48,000 pages bound into ninety-eight volumes of collected works—have been disaggregated and carried off, event by event, sentence by sentence, until no coherent narrative remains, if indeed there ever was one. The trouble is that Gandhi actually said everything and its opposite. To cherry pickers, he offers such a bewildering variety of cherries that you have to wonder if there was something the matter with the tree.

For example, there's his well-known description of an arcadian paradise in "The Pyramid vs. the Oceanic Circle", written in 1946:

> Independence begins at the bottom. Thus every village will be a republic or panchayat having full powers. It follows, therefore, that every village has to be self-sustained and capable of managing

its affairs even to the extent of defending itself against the whole world… In this structure composed of innumerable villages there will be ever-widening, never-ascending circles. Life will not be a pyramid with the apex sustained by the bottom. But it will be an oceanic circle whose centre will be the individual always ready to perish for the village… Therefore the outermost circumference will not wield power to crush the inner circle but will give strength to all within and derive its own strength from it.[55]

Then there is his endorsement of the caste system in 1921 in *Navajivan*. It is translated from Gujarati by Ambedkar (who suggested more than once that Gandhi "deceived" people, and that his writings in English and Gujarati could be productively compared):[56]

Caste is another name for control. Caste puts a limit on enjoyment. Caste does not allow a person to transgress caste limits in pursuit of his enjoyment. That is the meaning of such caste restrictions as inter-dining and inter-marriage… These being my views I am opposed to all those who are out to destroy the Caste System.[57]

Is this not the very antithesis of "ever-widening and never-ascending circles"?

It's true that these statements were made twenty-five years apart. Does that mean that Gandhi reformed? That he changed his views on caste? He did, at a glacial pace. From believing in the caste system in all its minutiae, he moved to saying that the four thousand separate castes should 'fuse' themselves into the four varnas (what Ambedkar called the 'parent' of the caste system). Towards the end of Gandhi's life (when his views were just views and did not run the risk of translating into political action), he said that he no longer objected to inter-dining and intermarriage between castes. Sometimes he said that though he believed in the varna system, a person's varna ought to be decided by their worth and not their birth (which was also the Arya Samaj position). Ambedkar pointed out the absurdity of this idea: "How are you going to compel people who have acquired a higher status based on birth, without reference to their worth, to vacate that status? How are you going to compel people to recognise the status due to a man, in accordance to his worth, who is occupying a lower status based on his birth?"[58] He went on to ask what would happen to women, whether their status would be decided upon their own worth or their husbands' worth.

Notwithstanding stories and anecdotes from Gandhi's followers about Gandhi's love for Untouchables and the inter-caste weddings he attended, in the ninety-eight volumes of his writing, Gandhi never decisively and categorically renounced his belief in chaturvarna, the system of four varnas. Though he was given to apologising and agonising publicly and privately over things like the occasional lapses in his control over his sexual desire,[59] he never agonised over the extremely damaging things he had said and done on caste.

Still, why not eschew the negative and concentrate instead on what was good about Gandhi, use it to bring out the best in people? It is a valid question, and one that those who have built shrines to Gandhi have probably answered for themselves. After all, it is possible to admire the work of great composers, writers, architects, sportspersons and musicians whose views are inimical to our own. The difference is that Gandhi was not a composer or writer or musician or a sportsman. He offered himself to us as a visionary, a mystic, a moralist, a great humanitarian, the man who brought down a mighty empire armed only with Truth and Righteousness. How do we reconcile the idea of the non-violent Gandhi, the Gandhi who spoke Truth to Power, Gandhi the Nemesis of Injustice, the Gentle Gandhi, the Androgynous Gandhi, Gandhi the Mother, the Gandhi who (allegedly) feminised politics and created space for women to enter the political arena, the eco-Gandhi, the Gandhi of the ready wit and some great one-liners—how do we reconcile all this with Gandhi's views (and deeds) on caste? What do we do with this structure of moral righteousness that rests so comfortably on a foundation of utterly brutal, institutionalised injustice? Is it enough to say Gandhi was complicated, and let it go at that? There is no doubt that Gandhi was an extraordinary and fascinating man, but during India's struggle for freedom, did he really speak Truth to Power? Did he really ally himself with the poorest of the poor, the most vulnerable of his people?

"It is foolish to take solace in the fact that because the Congress is fighting for the freedom of India, it is, therefore, fighting for the freedom of the people of India and of the lowest of the low", Ambedkar said. "The question whether the Congress is fighting for freedom has very little importance as compared to the question for whose freedom is the Congress fighting".[60]

In 1931, when Ambedkar met Gandhi for the first time, Gandhi questioned him about his sharp criticism of the Congress (which, it was assumed, was tantamount to criticising the struggle for the Homeland). "Gandhiji, I have no Homeland", was Ambedkar's famous reply. "No Untouchable worth the name will be proud of this land".[61]

History has been unkind to Ambedkar. First it contained him, and then it glorified him. It has made him India's Leader of the Untouchables, the King of the Ghetto. It has hidden away his writings. It has stripped away the radical intellect and the searing insolence.

All the same, Ambedkar's followers have kept his legacy alive in creative ways. One of those ways is to turn him into a million mass-produced statues. The Ambedkar statue is a radical and animate object.[62] It has been sent forth into the world to claim the space—both physical and virtual, public and private—that is the Dalit's due. Dalits have used Ambedkar's statue to assert their civil rights—to claim land that is owed them, water that is theirs, commons they are denied access to. The Ambedkar statue that is planted on the commons and rallied around always holds a book in its hand. Significantly, that book is not *Annihilation of Caste* with its liberating, revolutionary rage. It is a copy of the Indian Constitution that Ambedkar played a vital role in conceptualising—the document that now, for better or for worse, governs the life of every single Indian citizen.

Using the Constitution as a subversive object is one thing. Being limited by it is quite another. Ambedkar's circumstances forced him to be a revolutionary and to simultaneously put his foot in the door of the establishment whenever he got a chance to. His genius lay in his ability to use both these aspects of himself nimbly, and to great effect. Viewed through the prism of the present, however, it has meant that he left behind a dual and sometimes confusing legacy: Ambedkar the Radical, and Ambedkar the Father of the Indian Constitution. Constitutionalism can come in the way of revolution. And the Dalit revolution has not happened yet. We still await it. Before that there cannot be any other, not in India.

This is not to suggest that writing a constitution cannot be a radical act. It can be, it could have been, and Ambedkar tried his best to make it one. However, by his own admission, he did not entirely succeed.

As India hurtled towards independence, both Ambedkar and Gandhi were seriously concerned about the fate of minorities, particularly Muslims and Untouchables, but they responded to the approaching birth of the new nation in very different ways. Gandhi distanced himself more and more from the business of nation building. For him, the Congress party's work was done. He wanted the party dissolved. He believed (quite rightly) that the state represented violence in a concentrated and organised form, that because it was not a human entity, because it was soulless, it owed its very existence to violence.[63] In Gandhi's understanding, swaraj (self-rule) lived in the moral heart of his people, though he made it clear that by 'his people' he did not mean the majority community alone:

> It has been said that Indian swaraj will be the rule of the majority community, i.e., the Hindus. There could not be a greater mistake than that. If it were to be true, I for one would refuse to call it swaraj and would fight it with all the strength at my command, for to me *Hind Swaraj* is the rule of all the people, is the rule of justice.[64]

For Ambedkar, "the people" was not a homogeneous category that glowed with the rosy hue of innate righteousness. He knew that, regardless of what Gandhi said, it would inevitably be the majority community that decided what form swaraj would take. The prospect of India's Untouchables being ruled by nothing other than the moral heart of India's predominantly Hindu people filled him with foreboding. Ambedkar became anxious, even desperate, to manoeuvre himself into becoming a member of the Constituent Assembly, a position that would enable him to influence the shape and the spirit of the Constitution for the emerging nation in real and practical ways. For this he was even prepared to set aside his pride, and his misgivings about his old foe, the Congress party.

Ambedkar's main concern was to privilege and legalise "constitutional morality" over the traditional, social morality of the caste system. Speaking in the Constituent Assembly on 4 November 1948, he said, "Constitutional morality is not a natural sentiment. It has to be cultivated. We must realise that our people have yet to learn it. Democracy in India is only a top-dressing on an Indian soil which is essentially undemocratic".[65]

Ambedkar was seriously disappointed with the final draft of the Constitution. Still, he did succeed in putting in place certain rights and safeguards that would, as far as the subordinated castes were concerned, make it a document that was more enlightened than the society it was drafted for. (For others, however, like India's Adivasis, the Constitution turned out to be just an extension of colonial practice. We'll come to that later.) Ambedkar thought of the Constitution as a work in progress. Like Thomas Jefferson, he believed that unless every generation had the right to create a new constitution for itself, the earth would belong to "the dead and not the living".[66] The trouble is that the living are not necessarily more progressive or enlightened than the dead. There are a number of forces today, political as well as commercial, that are lobbying to rewrite the Constitution in utterly regressive ways.

Though Ambedkar was a lawyer, he had no illusions about law-making. As Law Minister in post-independence India, he worked for months on a draft of the Hindu Code Bill. He believed that the caste system advanced itself by controlling women, and one of his major concerns was to make Hindu personal law more equitable for women.[67] The Bill he proposed sanctioned divorce and expanded the property rights of widows and daughters. The Constituent Assembly dragged its feet over it for four years (from 1947 to 1951) and then blocked it.[68] The President, Rajendra Prasad, threatened to stall the Bill's passage into law. Hindu sadhus laid siege to Parliament. Industrialists and zamindars warned they would withdraw their support in the coming elections.[69] Eventually Ambedkar resigned as Law Minister. In his resignation speech he said: "To leave inequality between class and class, between sex and sex, which is the soul of Hindu society, and to go on passing legislation relating to economic problems is to make a farce of our Constitution and to build a palace on a dung heap."[70]

More than anything else, what Ambedkar brought to a complicated, multifaceted political struggle, with more than its fair share of sectarianism, obscurantism and skulduggery, was intelligence.

▼

Annihilation of Caste is often called (even by some Ambedkarites) Ambedkar's utopia—his impracticable, unfeasible dream. He was rolling a boulder up a cliff, they say. How can a society so steeped in faith and superstition be expected to be open to such a ferocious attack on its most deeply held beliefs? After all, for millions of Hindus of all castes, including Untouchables, Hinduism in its practice is a way of life that pervades everything—birth, death, war, marriage, food, music, poetry, dance. It is their culture, their very identity. How can Hinduism be renounced only because the practice of caste is sanctioned in its foundational texts, which most people have never read?

Ambedkar's point is—how can it not be? How can such institutionalised injustice, even if it is divinely ordained, be acceptable to anyone?

> It is no use seeking refuge in quibbles. It is no use telling people that the shastras do not say what they are believed to say, if they are grammatically read or logically interpreted. What matters is how the shastras have been understood by people. You must take the stand that Buddha took... You must not only discard the shastras, you must deny their authority as did Buddha and Nanak. You must have the courage to tell the Hindus that what is wrong with them is their religion—the religion which has produced in them this notion of the sacredness of caste. Will you show that courage?[71]

Gandhi believed that Ambedkar was throwing the baby out with the bathwater. Ambedkar believed the baby and the bathwater were a single, fused organism.

Let us concede—but never accept—that *Annihilation of Caste* is indeed a piece of utopian thinking. If it is, then let us concede and accept how reduced, how depleted and how pitiable we would be as a people if even this—this rage, this audacious denunciation—did not exist in our midst. Ambedkar's anger gives us all a little shelter, a little dignity.

The utopianism that Ambedkar is charged with was very much part of the tradition of the anticaste movement. The poetry of the Bhakti movement is replete with it. Unlike the nostalgia-ridden, mythical village republics in Gandhi's 'Ram Rajya' (the reign of Lord Ram), the subaltern Bhakti sants sang of towns.[72] They sang of towns in timeless places, where Untouchables would be liberated from ubiquitous fear, from unimaginable indignity and endless toil on other peoples' land. For Ravidas (also known as Raidas, Ruhidas, Rohidas), that place was Be-gham-pura, the City without Sorrow, the city without segregation, where people were free to go wherever they wanted:

Where there is no affliction or suffering
Neither anxiety nor fear, taxes nor capital
No menace, no terror, no humiliation...
Says Raidas the emancipated Chamar:
One who shares with me that city is my friend.[73]

For Tukaram, the city was Pandharpur, where everybody was equal, where the headman had to work as hard as everyone else, where people danced and sang and mingled freely. For Kabir, it was Premnagar, the City of Love.

Ambedkar's utopia was a pretty hard-nosed one. It was, so to speak, the City of Justice—worldly justice. He imagined an enlightened India, Prabuddha Bharat, that fused the best ideas of the European Enlightenment with Buddhist thought. *Prabuddha Bharat* was, in fact, the name he gave to the last of the four newspapers he edited in his lifetime.

If Gandhi's radical critique of Western modernity came from a nostalgic evocation of a uniquely Indian pastoral bliss, Ambedkar's critique of that nostalgia came from an embrace of pragmatic Western liberalism and its definitions of progress and happiness. (Which, at this moment, is experiencing a crisis from which it may not recover.)

Gandhi called modern cities an "excrescence" that "served at the present moment the evil purpose of draining the life-blood of the villages".[74] To Ambedkar, and to most Dalits, Gandhi's ideal village was, understandably, "a sink of localism, a den of ignorance, narrow-mindedness and communalism".[75] The impetus towards justice turned Ambedkar's gaze away from the village towards the city, towards urbanism, modernism and industrialisation—big cities, big dams, big irrigation projects. Ironically, this is the very model of 'development' that hundreds of thousands of people today associate with injustice, a model that lays the environment to waste and involves the forcible displacement of millions of people from their villages and homes by mines, dams and other major infrastructural projects. Meanwhile, Gandhi—whose mythical village is so blind to appalling, inherent injustice—has, as ironically, become the talisman for these struggles for justice.

While Gandhi promoted his village republic, his pragmatism, or what some might call his duality, allowed him to support and be supported by big industry and big dams as well.[76]

The rival utopias of Gandhi and Ambedkar represented the classic battle between tradition and modernity. If utopias can be said to be 'right' and 'wrong', then both were right, and both were also grievously wrong. Gandhi was prescient enough to recognise the seed of cataclysm that was implanted in the project of Western modernity:

> God forbid that India should ever take to industrialism after the manner of the West. The economic imperialism of a single tiny island kingdom is today keeping the world in chains. If an entire nation of 300 millions took to similar economic exploitation it would strip the world bare like locusts.[77]

As the earth warms up, as glaciers melt and forests disappear, Gandhi's words have turned out to be prophetic. But his horror of modern civilisation led him to eulogise a mythical Indian past that was, in his telling, just and beautiful. Ambedkar, on his part, was painfully aware of the iniquity of that past, but in his urgency to move away from it, he failed to recognise the catastrophic dangers of Western modernity.

Ambedkar's and Gandhi's very different utopias ought not to be appraised or assessed by the 'end product' alone—the village or the city. Equally important is the impetus that drove those utopias. For Ambedkarites to call mass struggles against contemporary models of development 'eco-romantic' and for Gandhians to hold Gandhi out as a symbol of justice and moral virtue are shallow interpretations of the very different passions that drove the two men.

The towns the Bhakti poet-saints dreamed of—Beghampura, Pandharpur, Premnagar—had one thing in common. They all existed in a time and space that was liberated from the bonds of Brahminism. Brahminism was the term that the anticaste movement preferred over 'Hinduism'. By Brahminism, they didn't mean Brahmins as a caste or a community. They meant the domino effect, what Ambedkar called the "infection of imitation", that the caste that first "enclosed" itself—the Brahmins—set off. "Some closed the door," he wrote, "others found it closed against them".[78]

The "infection of imitation", like the half-life of a radioactive atom, decays exponentially as it moves down the caste ladder, but never quite disappears. It has created what Ambedkar describes as a system of "graded inequality" in which "there is no such class as a completely unprivileged class except the one which is at the base of the social pyramid. The privileges of the rest are graded. Even the low is privileged as compared with lower. Each class being privileged, every class is interested in maintaining the system".[79]

The exponential decay of the radioactive atom of caste means that Brahminism is practised not just by the Brahmin against the Kshatriya or the Vaishya against the Shudra, or the Shudra against the Untouchable, but also by the Untouchable against the Unapproachable, the Unapproachable against the Unseeable. It means there is a quotient of Brahminism in everybody, regardless of which caste they belong to. It is the ultimate means of control in which the concept of pollution and purity and the perpetration of social as well as physical violence—an inevitable part of administering an oppressive hierarchy—is not just outsourced, but implanted in everybody's imagination, including those at the bottom of the hierarchy. It's like an elaborate enforcement network in which everybody polices everybody else. The Unapproachable polices the Unseeable, the Malas resent the Madigas, the Madigas turn upon the Dakkalis, who sit on the Rellis; the Vanniyars quarrel with the Paraiyars, who in turn could beat up the Arundhatiyars.

Brahminism makes it impossible to draw a clear line between victims and oppressors, even though the hierarchy of caste makes it more than clear that there are victims and oppressors. (The line between Touchables and Untouchables, for example, is dead clear.) Brahminism precludes the possibility of social or political solidarity across caste lines. As an administrative system, it is pure genius. "A single spark can light a prairie fire" was Mao Zedong's famous message to his guerrilla army. Perhaps. But Brahminism has given us in India a labyrinth instead of a prairie. And the poor little single spark wanders, lost in a warren of firewalls. Brahminism, Ambedkar said, "is the very negation of the spirit of Liberty, Equality and Fraternity".[80]

▼

Annihilation of Caste is the text of a speech Ambedkar was supposed to deliver in Lahore in 1936 to an audience of privileged-caste

Hindus. The organisation that had been bold enough to invite him to deliver its presidential address was the Jat-Pat Todak Mandal (Forum for Break-up of Caste) of Lahore, a 'radical' offshoot of the Arya Samaj. Most of its members were privileged-caste Hindu reformers. They asked to be provided the text of the speech in advance, so that they could print and distribute it. When they read it and realised that Ambedkar was going to launch an intellectual assault on the Vedas and shastras, on Hinduism itself, they wrote to him:

> [T]hose of us who would like to see the conference terminate without any untoward incident would prefer that at least the word 'Veda' be left out for the time being. I leave this to your good sense. I hope, however, in your concluding paragraphs you will make it clear that the views expressed in the address are your own and that the responsibility does not lie on the Mandal.[81]

Ambedkar refused to alter his speech, and so the event was cancelled. His text ought not to have come as such a surprise to the Mandal. Just a few months previously, on 13 October 1935, at the Depressed Classes Conference in Yeola in the Bombay Presidency (now in the state of Maharashtra), Ambedkar had told an audience of more than ten thousand people:

> Because we have the misfortune of calling ourselves Hindus, we are treated thus. If we were members of another faith none would treat us so. Choose any religion which gives you equality of status and treatment. We shall repair our mistake now. I had the misfortune of being born with the stigma of an Untouchable. However, it is not my fault; but I will not die a Hindu, for this is in my power.[82]

At that particular moment in time, the threat of religious conversion by an Untouchable leader of Ambedkar's standing came as the worst possible news to Hindu reformers.

Conversion was by no means new. Seeking to escape the

stigma of caste, Untouchable and other degraded labouring castes had begun to convert to other religions centuries ago. Millions had converted to Islam during the years of Muslim rule. Later, millions more had taken to Sikhism and Christianity. (Sadly, caste prejudice in the subcontinent trumps religious belief. Though their scriptures do not sanction it, elite Indian Muslims, Sikhs and Christians all practise caste discrimination.[83] Pakistan, Bangladesh and Nepal all have their own communities of Untouchable sweepers. So does Kashmir. But that's another story.)

The mass conversion of oppressed-caste Hindus, particularly to Islam, continues to sit uncomfortably with Hindu supremacist history writing, which dwells on a golden age of Hinduism that was brought to naught by the cruelty and vandalism of Muslim rule.[84] Vandalism and cruelty there certainly was. Yet it meant different things to different people. Here is Jotiba Phule (1827–90), the earliest of the modern anticaste intellectuals, on the subject of the Muslim rule and of the so-called golden age of the Arya Bhats (Brahmins):

> The Muslims, destroying the carved stone images of the cunning Arya Bhats, forcibly enslaved them and brought the Shudras and Ati-Shudras in great numbers out of their clutches and made them Muslims, including them in the Muslim Religion. Not only this, but they established inter-dining and intermarriage with them and gave them all equal rights. They made them all as happy as themselves and forced the Arya Bhats to see all this.[85]

By the turn of the century, however, religious conversion came to have completely different implications in India. A new set of unfamiliar considerations entered the mix. Opposing an unpopular regime was no longer just a question of a conquering army riding into the capital, overthrowing the monarch and taking the throne. The old idea of empire was metamorphosing into the new idea of the nation state. Modern governance now involved addressing the volatile question of the right to representation: who had the right to represent the Indian people? The Hindus, the Muslims, the Sikhs, the Christians, the privileged castes, the oppressed castes, the farmers, the workers? How would the 'self' in self-rule—the 'swa' in swaraj—be constituted? Who would decide? Suddenly, a people who belonged to an impossibly diverse range of races, castes, tribes and religions—who, between them, spoke more than one thousand languages—had to be transformed into modern citizens of a modern nation. The process of synthetic homogenisation began to have the opposite effect. Even as the modern Indian nation constituted itself, it began to fracture.

Under the new dispensation, demography became vitally important. The empirical taxonomy of the British census had solidified and freeze-dried the rigid but not entirely inflexible hierarchy of caste, adding its own prejudices and value judgements to the mix, classifying entire communities as 'criminals' and 'warriors' and so on. The Untouchable castes were entered under the accounting head 'Hindu'. (In 1930, according to Ambedkar, the Untouchables numbered about 44.5 million.[86] The population of African Americans in the US around the same time was 8.8 million.) The large-scale exodus of Untouchables from the 'Hindu fold' would have been catastrophic for the 'Hindu' majority. In pre-partition, undivided Punjab, for example, between 1881 and 1941, the Hindu population dropped from 43.8 per cent to 29.1 per cent, due largely to the conversion of the subordinated castes to Islam, Sikhism and Christianity.[87]

Hindu reformers hurried to stem this migration. The Arya Samaj, founded in 1875 in Lahore by Dayananda Saraswati (born Mool Shankar, a Gujarati Brahmin from Kathiawar), was one of the earliest. It preached against the practice of untouchability and banned idol worship. Dayananda Saraswati initiated the Shuddhi programme in 1877, to 'purify the impure', and, in the early twentieth century, his disciples took this up on a mass scale in North India.

In 1899, Swami Vivekananda of the Ramakrishna Math—the man who became famous in 1893 when he addressed the Parliament of the World's Religions in Chicago in his sadhu's robes—said, "Every man going out of the Hindu pale is not only a man less, but an enemy the more".[88] A raft of new reformist outfits appeared in Punjab, committed to saving Hinduism by winning the 'hearts and minds' of Untouchables: the Shradhananda Dalituddhar Sabha, the All-India Achhutodhar Committee, the Punjab Achhut Udhar Mandal[89] and the Jat-Pat Todak Mandal which was part of the Arya Samaj.

The reformers' use of the words 'Hindu' and 'Hinduism' was new. Until then, they had been used by the British as well as the Mughals, but it was not the way people who were described as Hindus chose to describe themselves. Until the panic over demography began, they had always foregrounded their jati, their caste identity. "The first and foremost thing that must be recognised is that Hindu society is a myth. The name Hindu is itself a foreign name", said Ambedkar.

> It was given by the Mohammedans to the natives [who lived east of the river Indus] for the purpose of distinguishing themselves. It does not occur in any Sanskrit work prior to the Mohammedan invasion. They did not feel the necessity of a common name, because they had no conception of their having constituted a community. Hindu society as such does not exist. It is only a collection of castes.[90]

When reformers began to use the word 'Hindu' to describe themselves and their organisations, it had less to do with religion than with trying to forge a unified political constitution out of a divided people. This explains the reformers' constant references to the 'Hindu nation' or the 'Hindu race'.[91] This political Hinduism later came to be called Hindutva.[92]

The issue of demography was addressed openly, and head-on. "In this country, the government is based on numbers", wrote the editor of *Pratap*, a Kanpur newspaper, on 10 January 1921.

> Shuddhi has become a matter of life and death for Hindus. The Muslims have grown from negative quantity into 70 million. The Christians number four million. 220 million Hindus are finding it hard to live because of 70 million Muslims. If their numbers increase only God knows what will happen. It is true that Shuddhi should be for religious purposes alone, but the Hindus have been obliged by other considerations as well to embrace their other brothers. If the Hindus do not wake up now, they will be finished.[93]

Conservative Hindu organisations like the Hindu Mahasabha took the task beyond rhetoric, and against their own deeply held beliefs and practice began to proselytise energetically against untouchability. Untouchables had to be prevented from defecting. They had to be assimilated, their proteins broken down. They had to be brought into the Big House, but kept in the servants' quarters. Here is Ambedkar on the subject:

> It is true that Hinduism can absorb many things. The beef-eating Hinduism (or strictly speaking Brahminism which is the proper name of Hinduism in its earlier stage) absorbed the non-violence theory of Buddhism and became a religion of vegetarianism. But there is one thing which Hinduism has never been able to do—namely to adjust itself to absorb the Untouchables or to remove the bar of untouchability.[94]

While the Hindu reformers went about their business, anticaste movements led by Untouchables began to organise themselves too. Swami Achhutanand Harihar presented the Prince of Wales with a charter of seventeen demands including land reform, separate schools for Untouchable children and separate electorates. Another well-known figure was Babu Mangoo Ram. He was a member of the revolutionary, anti-imperialist Ghadar Party established in 1913, predominantly by Punjabi migrants in the United States and Canada. Ghadar (Revolt) was an international movement of Punjabi Indians who had been inspired by the 1857 Mutiny, also called the First War of Independence. Its aim was to overthrow the British by means of armed struggle. (It was, in some ways, India's first communist party. Unlike the Congress, which had an urban, privileged-caste leadership, the Ghadar Party was closely linked to the Punjab peasantry. Though it has ceased to exist, its memory continues to be a rallying point for several left-wing revolutionary parties in Punjab.) However, when Babu Mangoo Ram returned to India after a decade in the United States, the caste system was waiting for him. He found he was Untouchable again.[95] In 1926, he founded the Ad Dharm movement, with Ravidas, the Bhakti sant, as its spiritual hero. Ad Dharmis declared that they were neither Sikh nor Hindu. Many Untouchables left the Arya Samaj to join the Ad Dharm movement.[96] Babu Mangoo Ram went on to become a comrade of Ambedkar's.

The anxiety over demography made for turbulent politics. There were other lethal games afoot. The British government had given itself the right to rule India by imperial fiat and had consolidated its power by working closely with the Indian elite, taking care never to upset the status quo.[97] It had drained the wealth of a once-wealthy subcontinent—or, shall we say, drained the wealth of the elite in a once-wealthy subcontinent. It had caused famines in which millions had died while the British government exported food to England.[98] None of that stopped it from also lighting sly fires that ignited caste and communal tension. In 1905, it partitioned Bengal along communal lines. In 1909, it passed the Morley–Minto reforms, granting Muslims a separate electorate in the Central as well as Provincial Legislative Councils. It began to question the moral and political legitimacy of anybody who opposed it. How could a people who practised something as primitive as untouchability talk of self-rule? How could the Congress party, run by elite, privileged-caste Hindus, claim to represent the Muslims? Or the Untouchables? Coming from the British government, it was surely wicked, but even wicked questions need answers.

The person who stepped into the widening breach was perhaps the most consummate politician the modern world has ever known—Mohandas Karamchand Gandhi. If the British had their imperial mandate to raise them above the fray, Gandhi had his Mahatmahood.

▼

Gandhi returned to India in 1915 after twenty years of political activity in South Africa, and plunged into the national movement. His first concern, as any politician's would be, was to stitch together the various constituencies that would allow the Indian National Congress to claim it was the legitimate and sole representative of the emerging nation. It was a formidable task. The temptations and contradictions of attempting to represent everybody—Hindus, Muslims, Christians, Sikhs, privileged castes, subordinated castes, peasants, farmers, serfs, zamindars, workers and industrialists—were all absorbed into the other-worldly provenance of Gandhi's Mahatmahood.

Like Shiva in the myth, who swallowed poison to save the world in the story of the Samudra Manthan—the churning of the Ocean of Milk—Gandhi stood foremost among his peers and fellow-churners, and tried to swallow the poison that rose up from the depths as he helped to roil the new nation into existence. Unfortunately, Gandhi was not Shiva, and the poison eventually overwhelmed him. The greater the Congress party's impulse to hegemony, the more violently things blew apart. The three main constituencies it had to win over were the conservative, privileged-caste Hindus, the Untouchables and the Muslims.

For the conservative Hindus, the Congress party's natural constituency, Gandhi held aloft the utopia of Ram Rajya and the *Bhagvad Gita*, his "spiritual dictionary". (It's the book most Gandhi statues hold.) He called himself a "Sanatani Hindu". Sanatan dharma, by virtue of being 'eternal law', positions itself as the origin of all things, the 'container' of everything. Spiritually, it is a generous and beautiful idea, the very epitome of tolerance and pluralism. Politically, it is used in the opposite way, for the very narrow purpose of assimilation and domination, in which all religions—Islam, Buddhism, Jainism, Sikhism, Christianity—are sought to be absorbed. They're expected to function like small concerns under the umbrella of a larger holding company.

To woo its second major constituency, the Untouchables, the Indian National Congress passed a resolution in 1917 abolishing untouchability. Annie Besant of the Theosophical Society, a founding member of the Congress, presided over the meeting. Ambedkar called it "a strange event".[99] He republished Besant's essay published in the *Indian Review* in 1909, in which she had made a case for segregating Untouchable children from the children of 'purer' castes in schools:

> Their bodies at present are ill-odorous and foul with the liquor and strong-smelling food out of which for generations they have been built up; it will need some generations of purer food and living to make their bodies fit to sit in the close neighbourhood of a school room with children who have received bodies trained in

habits of exquisite personal cleanliness and fed on pure food stuffs. We have to raise the Depressed Classes to a similar level of purity, not drag the clean to the level of the dirty, and until that is done, close association is undesirable.[100]

The third big constituency the Congress party needed to address was the Muslims (who, for caste Hindus, counted on the purity–pollution scale as *mleccha*—impure; sharing food and water with them was forbidden). In 1920, the Congress decided to ally with conservative Indian Muslims who were leading the pan-Islamist agitation against the partitioning of the Ottoman territories by the Allies after the First World War. The Sultan of the defeated Ottomans was the Caliph, the spiritual head of Sunni Islam. Sunni Muslims equated the partition of the Ottoman Empire with a threat to the Islamic Caliphate itself. Led by Gandhi, the Congress party leapt into the fray and included the Khilafat (Caliphate) agitation in its first national satyagraha. The satyagraha had been planned to protest the Rowlatt Act passed in 1919 to extend the British government's wartime emergency powers.

Whether or not Gandhi's support for the Khilafat movement was just ordinary political opportunism is a subject that has been debated endlessly. The historian Faisal Devji argues convincingly that at this point Gandhi was acting with a certain internationalism; as a responsible 'imperial subject' (which was how he saw himself in his years in South Africa), he was attempting to morally transform Empire and hold it accountable to all its subjects.[101] Gandhi called Khilafat an "ideal" and asked that the struggle of "Non-cooperation be recognised as a struggle of 'religion against irreligion'".[102] By this he meant that Hinduism and Islam should join forces to transform a Christianity that, as Gandhi saw it, was losing its moral core. It was during the first Non-Cooperation Movement that Gandhi made religion and religious symbolism the central tenet of his politics. Perhaps he thought he was lighting a wayside fire for pilgrims to warm their souls. But it ended in a blaze that has still not been put out.

By expressing solidarity with a pan-Islamic movement, Gandhi was throwing his turban into a much larger ring. Though he went to great lengths to underline his 'Hinduness', he was staking his claim to be more than just a Hindu or even an Indian leader—he was aspiring to be the leader of all the subjects of the British Empire. Gandhi's support for Khilafat, however, played straight into the hands of Hindu extremists, who had by then begun to claim that Muslims were not 'true' Indians because the centre of gravity of Muslim fealty lay outside of India. The Congress party's alliance with conservative Muslims angered conservative Hindus as well as moderate Muslims.

In 1922, when the Non-Cooperation Movement was at its peak, things went out of control. A mob killed twenty-two policemen and burnt down a police station in Chauri Chaura in the United Provinces (today's Uttar Pradesh). Gandhi saw this violence as a sign that people had not yet evolved into true satyagrahis, that they were not ready for non-violence and non-cooperation. Without consulting any other leaders, Gandhi unilaterally called off the satyagraha. Since the Non-Cooperation Movement and the Khilafat movement were conjoined, it meant an end to the Khilafat movement too. Infuriated by this arbitrariness, the leaders of the Khilafat movement parted ways with the Congress. Things began to unravel.

By 1925, Dr K.B. Hedgewar had founded the Rashtriya Swayamsevak Sangh (RSS), a Hindu nationalist organisation. B.S. Moonje, one of the early ideologues of the RSS, travelled to Italy in 1931 and met Mussolini. Inspired by European fascism, the RSS began to create its own squads of storm troopers. (Today they number in the millions. RSS members include former Prime Minister Atal Bihari Vajpayee, former Home Minister L.K. Advani, and four-time Chief Minister of Gujarat Narendra

Modi.) By the time the Second World War broke out, Hitler and Mussolini were the RSS's spiritual and political leaders (and so they still remain). The RSS subsequently declared that India was a Hindu nation and that Muslims in India were the equivalent of the Jews in Germany. In 1939, M.S. Golwalkar, who succeeded Hedgewar as the head of the RSS, wrote in what is regarded as the RSS bible, *We, or Our Nationhood Defined*:

> To keep up the purity of its race and culture, Germany shocked the world by purging the country of the semitic races—the Jews. Race pride at its highest has been manifested here ... a good lesson for us in Hindustan to learn and profit by.[103]

By 1940, the Muslim League, led by M.A. Jinnah, had passed the Pakistan Resolution.

In 1947, in what must surely count as one of the most callous, iniquitous acts in history, the British government drew a hurried border through the country that cut through communities and people, villages and homes, with less care than it might have taken to slice up a leg of lamb.

Gandhi, the Apostle of Peace and Non-violence, lived to see the movement he thought he led dissolve into a paroxysm of genocidal violence in which half a million people (a million, according to Stanley Wolpert in *A New History of India*) lost their lives and almost twelve million lost their homes, their past and everything they had ever known. Through the horror of partition, Gandhi did all he could to still the madness and bloodlust. He travelled deep into the very heart of the violence. He prayed, he pleaded, he fasted, but the incubus had been unleashed and could not be recalled. The hatred spilled over and consumed everything that came in its path. It continues to branch out, over-ground and underground. It has bequeathed the subcontinent a dangerous, deeply wounded psyche.

Amidst the frenzy of killing, ethnic cleansing and chest-thumping religious fundamentalism on both sides, the Government of Pakistan kept its head about one thing: it declared that Untouchable municipal sweepers were part of the country's 'essential services' and impounded them, refusing them permission to move to India. (Who else was going to clean people's shit in the Land of the Pure?) Ambedkar raised the matter with Prime Minister Jawaharlal Nehru in a letter in December 1947.[104] With great difficulty Ambedkar managed to help at least a section of the 'essential services' get across the border. Even today in Pakistan, while various Islamist sects slaughter each other over who is the better, more correct, more faithful Muslim, there does not seem to be much heartache over the very un-Islamic practice of untouchability.

Five months after partition, in January 1948, Gandhi was shot dead at a prayer meeting on the lawns of Birla House, where he usually lived when he visited Delhi. His assassin was Nathuram Godse, a Brahmin, and a former activist of the Hindu Mahasabha and the RSS. Godse was, if such a thing is possible, a most respectful assassin. First he saluted Gandhi for the work he had done to 'awaken' people, and then he shot him. After pulling the trigger, he stood his ground. He made no attempt to escape or to kill himself. In his book, *Why I Assassinated Mahatma Gandhi*, he said:

> [But] in India communal franchise, separate electorates and the like had already undermined the solidarity of the nation, more of such were in the offing and the sinister policy of communal favouritism was being pursued by the British with the utmost tenacity and without any scruple. Gandhiji therefore found it most difficult to obtain the unquestioned leadership of the Hindus and Muslims as in South Africa. But he had been accustomed to be the leader of all Indians. And quite frankly he could not understand the leadership of a divided country. It was absurd for his honest mind to think of accepting the generalship of any army divided against itself.[105]

Gandhi's assassin seemed to feel that he was saving the Mahatma from himself. Godse and his accomplice, Narayan Apte, climbed the gallows carrying a saffron flag, a map of undivided India and, ironically, a copy of the *Bhagvad Gita*, Gandhi's "spiritual dictionary".

The *Gita*, essentially Krishna's counsel to Arjuna during the battle of the Mahabharata (in which brothers fought brothers), is a philosophical and theological treatise on devotion and ethical practice on a battlefield. Ambedkar wasn't enamoured of the *Bhagvad Gita*. His view was that the *Gita* contained "an unheard of defence of murder". He called it a book that "offers a philosophic basis to the theory of Chaturvarna by linking it to the theory of innate, inborn qualities in men".[106]

Mahatma Gandhi died a sad and defeated man. Ambedkar was devastated. He wanted his adversary exposed, not killed. The country went into shock.

All that came later. We're getting ahead of the story.

▼

For more than thirty-five years before that, Gandhi's Mahatmahood had billowed like a sail in the winds of the national movement. He captured the world's imagination. He roused hundreds of thousands of people into direct political action. He was the cynosure of all eyes, the voice of the nation. In 1931, at the Second Round Table Conference in London, Gandhi claimed—with complete equanimity—that he represented all of India. In his first public confrontation with Ambedkar (over Ambedkar's proposal for a separate electorate for Untouchables), Gandhi felt able to say, "I claim myself in my own person to represent the vast mass of Untouchables."[107]

How could a privileged-caste Bania claim that he, in his own person, represented forty-five million Indian Untouchables unless he believed he actually was a Mahatma? Mahatmahood provided Gandhi with an amplitude that was not available to ordinary mortals. It allowed him to use his 'inner voice' affectively, effectively, and often. It allowed him the bandwidth to make daily broadcasts on the state of his hygiene, his diet, his bowel movements, his enemas and his sex life, and to draw the public into a net of prurient intimacy that he could then use and manipulate when he embarked on his fasts and other public acts of self-punishment. It permitted him to contradict himself constantly and then say: "My aim is not to be consistent with my previous statements on a given question, but to be consistent with the truth as it may present itself to me in a given moment. The result has been that I have grown from truth to truth".[108]

Ordinary politicians oscillate from political expediency to political expediency. A Mahatma can grow from truth to truth.

How did Gandhi come to be called a Mahatma? Did he begin with the compassion and egalitarian instincts of a saint? Did they come to him along the way?

In his recent biography of Gandhi, the historian Rama-chandra Guha argues that it was the two decades he spent working in South Africa that made Gandhi a Mahatma.[109] His canonisation—the first time he was publicly called Mahatma—was in 1915, soon after he returned from South Africa to begin work in India, at a meeting in Gondal, close to his hometown, Porbandar, in Gujarat.[110] At the time, few in India knew more than some very sketchy, rather inaccurate accounts of the struggles he had been engaged in. These need to be examined in some detail because whether or not they made him a Mahatma, they certainly shaped and defined his views on caste, race and imperialism. His views on race presaged his views on caste. What happened in South Africa continues to have serious implications for the Indian community there. Fortunately, we have the Mahatma's own words (and inconsistencies) to give us the detail and texture of those years.[111] To generations who have been raised on a diet of Gandhi hagiographies (including myself), to learn of what happened in South Africa is not just disturbing, it is almost stupefying.

THE SHINING PATH

Gandhi, twenty-four years old and trained as a lawyer in London's Inner Temple, arrived in South Africa in May 1893. He had a job as legal adviser to a wealthy Gujarati Muslim merchant. Imperial Britain was tightening its grip on the African continent. Gandhi was unkindly jolted into political awakening a few months after he arrived. Half the story is legendary: Gandhi was thrown out of a 'Whites only' first-class coach of a train in Pietermaritzburg. The other half of the story is less known: Gandhi was not offended by racial segregation. He was offended that 'passenger Indians'—Indian merchants who were predominantly Muslim but also privileged-caste Hindus—who had come to South Africa to do business, were being treated on a par with native Black Africans. Gandhi's argument was that passenger Indians came to Natal as British subjects and were entitled to equal treatment on the basis of Queen Victoria's 1858 proclamation, which asserted the equality of all imperial subjects.

In 1894, he became secretary of the Natal Indian Congress founded and funded by rich Indian merchants and traders. The membership fee, of three pounds,was a princely sum that meant the NIC would remain an elite club. (For a sense of proportion— twelve years later, the Zulus would rise in rebellion against the British for imposing an unaffordable one-pound poll tax on them.)

One of the earliest political victories for the NIC came in 1895 with a 'solution' to what was known as the Durban Post Office problem. The Post Office had only two entrances: one for Blacks and one for Whites. Gandhi petitioned the authorities and had a third entrance opened so that Indians did not need to use the same entrance as the 'Kaffirs'.[113] In an open letter to the Natal Legislative Assembly dated 19 December 1894, he says that both the English and the Indians "spring from common stock, called the Indo-Aryan", and cites Max Müller, Arthur Schopenhauer and William Jones to buttress his argument. He complains that the "Indian is being dragged down to the position of a raw Kaffir".[114] As spokesman for the Indian community, Gandhi was always careful to distinguish—and distance—passenger Indians from indentured (bonded) workers:

> Whether they are Hindus or Mahommedans, they are absolutely without any moral or religious instruction worthy of the name. They have not learned enough to educate themselves without any outside help. Placed thus, they are apt to yield to the slightest temptation to tell a lie. After some time, lying with them becomes a habit and a disease. They would lie without any reason, without any prospect of bettering themselves materially, indeed, without knowing what they are doing. They reach a stage in life when their moral faculties have completely collapsed owing to neglect.[115]

The Indian indentured labour whose "moral faculties" were in such a state of collapse were largely from the subordinated castes and lived and worked in conditions of virtual slavery, incarcerated on sugarcane farms. They were flogged, starved, imprisoned, often sexually abused, and died in great numbers.[116]

Gandhi soon became the most prominent spokesperson for the cause of the passenger Indians. In 1896, he travelled to India where he addressed packed—and increasingly indignant—meetings about the racism that Indians were being subjected to in South Africa. At the time, the White regime was getting increasingly anxious about the rapidly expanding Indian population. For them Gandhi was the leader of the 'coolies'—their name for all Indians.[117] In a perverse sense, their racism was inclusive. It didn't notice the distinctions that Gandhi went to such great lengths to make.

When Gandhi returned to Durban in January 1897, the news of his campaign had preceded him. His ship was met by thousands of hostile White demonstrators, who refused to let it dock. It took several days of negotiation before Gandhi was allowed to disembark. On his way home, on 12 January 1897, he was attacked and beaten. He bore the attack with fortitude and dignity.[118] Two days later, in an interview with the *Natal Advertiser*, Gandhi once again distanced himself from the 'coolies':

> I have said most emphatically, in the pamphlets and elsewhere, that the treatment of the indentured Indians is no worse or better in Natal than they receive in any other parts of the world. I have never endeavoured to show that the indentured Indians have been receiving cruel treatment.[119]

In 1899, the British went to war with Dutch settlers over the spoils of South Africa. Diamonds had been discovered in Kimberley in 1870, and gold on the Witwatersrand in 1886. The Anglo-Boer War, as it was called then, is known more properly today as the South African War or the White Man's War. Thousands of Black Africans and indentured Indian labourers were dragooned into the armies on either side. The Indians were not given arms, so they worked as menials and stretcher-bearers. Gandhi and a band of passenger Indians, who felt it was their responsibility as imperial subjects, volunteered their services to the British. Gandhi was enlisted in the Ambulance Corps.

It was a brutal war in which British troops fought Boer guerrillas. The British burnt down thousands of Boer farms, slaughtering people and cattle as they swept through the land. Tens of thousands of Boer civilians, mostly women and children, were moved into concentration camps, in which almost thirty thousand people died. Many simply starved to death.[120] These concentration camps were the first of their kind, the progenitors of Hitler's extermination camps for Jews. Several years later, after he returned to India, when Gandhi wrote about the South African war in his memoirs, he suggested that the prisoners in the camps were practising a cheerful form of satyagraha (which was the course of action he prescribed to the Jews of Germany too):[121]

> Boer women understood that their religion required them to suffer in order to preserve their independence, and therefore, patiently and cheerfully endured all hardships... They starved, they suffered biting cold and scorching heat. Sometimes a soldier intoxicated by liquor or maddened by passion might even assault these unprotected women. Still the brave women did not flinch.[122]

After the war, the British announced that their troops would be given a slab each of "Queen's Chocolate" as a reward for their bravery. Gandhi wrote a letter to the Colonial Secretary to ask for the largesse to be extended to the Ambulance Corps leaders, who had volunteered without pay: "It will be greatly appreciated by them and prized as a treasure if the terms under which the gift has been graciously made by Her Majesty would allow of its distribution among the Indian leaders."[123] The Colonial Secretary replied curtly to say that the chocolate was only for non-commissioned officers.

In 1901, with the Boer War now behind him, Gandhi spoke of how the objective of the Natal Indian Congress was to achieve a better understanding between the English and the Indians. He said he was looking forward to an "Imperial Brotherhood", towards which "everyone who was the friend of the Empire should aim".[124]

This was not to be. The Boers managed to outmanoeuvre and out-brotherhood Gandhi. In 1902, they signed the Treaty of Vereeniging with the British. According to the treaty, the Boer republics of the Transvaal and the Orange Free State became colonies of the British Empire under the sovereignty of the British Crown. In return, the British government agreed to give the colonies self-rule. The Boers became the British government's brutal lieutenants. Jan Smuts, once a dreaded Boer 'terrorist', switched sides and eventually led the British Army of South Africa in the First World War. The White folks made peace. They divided the diamonds, the gold and the land between themselves. Blacks, Indians and 'coloureds' were left out of the equation.

Gandhi was not deterred. A few years after the South African War, he once again volunteered for active service.

In 1906, the Zulu chief Bambatha kaMancinza led his people in an uprising against the British government's newly imposed one-pound poll tax. The Zulus and the British were old enemies and had fought each other before. In 1879, the Zulus had routed the British Army when it attacked the Zulu kingdom, a victory that put the Zulu on the world map. Eventually, over the years, because they could not match the firepower of British troops, they were conquered and driven off their land. Still, they refused to work on the White man's farms; which is why bonded, indentured labour was shipped in from India. Time and again, the Zulus had risen up. During the Bambatha Rebellion, the rebels, armed only with spears and cowhide shields, fought British troops equipped with modern artillery.

As the news of the rebellion came in, Gandhi published a series of letters in *Indian Opinion*, a Gujarati–English newspaper he had started in 1903. (One of its chief benefactors was Sir Ratanji Jamsetji Tata of the Tata industrial empire.) In a letter dated 18 November 1905, Gandhi said:

> At the time of the Boer War, it will be remembered, the Indians volunteered to do any work that might be entrusted to them, and it was with great difficulty that they could get their services accepted even for ambulance work. General Butler has certified

as to what kind of work the Natal Indian Volunteer Ambulance Corps did. If the Government only realised what reserve force is being wasted, they would make use of it and would give Indians a thorough training for actual warfare.[125]

On 14 April 1906, Gandhi wrote again in *Indian Opinion* (translated from Gujarati):

> What is our duty during these calamitous times in the Colony? It is not for us to say whether the revolt of the Kaffirs [Zulus] is justified or not. We are in Natal by virtue of British Power. Our very existence depends on it. It is therefore our duty to render whatever help we can. There was a discussion in the Press as to what part the Indian community would play in the event of an actual war. We have already declared in the English columns of this journal that the Indian community is prepared to play its part; and we believe what we did during the Boer War should also be done now.[126]

The rebellion was eventually contained. Chief Bambatha was captured and beheaded. Four thousand Zulus were killed, thousands more flogged and imprisoned. Even Winston Churchill, Master of War, at the time Under Secretary of State, was disturbed by the violence. He said: "It is my duty to warn the Secretary of State that this further disgusting butchery will excite in all probability great disapproval in the House of Commons... The score between black and white stands at present at about 3500 to 8."[127]

Gandhi, on his part, never regretted the role he played in the White Man's War and in the Bambatha uprising. He just reimagined it. Years later, in 1928, in *Satyagraha in South Africa*,[128] the memoirs he wrote in Yerawada Central Jail, both stories had, shall we say, evolved. By then the chessmen on the board had moved around. Gandhi had turned against the British. In his new account, the 'Truth' about the stretcher-bearer corps in the Bambatha Rebellion had 'grown' into another 'Truth':

The Zulu 'rebellion' broke out just while attempts were being made to impose further disabilities upon Indians in the Transvaal ... therefore I made an offer to the Government to raise a Stretcher-bearer Corps for service with the troops... The corps was on active service for a month... We had to cleanse the wounds of several Zulus which had not been attended to for as many as five or six days and were therefore stinking horribly. We liked the work. The Zulus could not talk to us, but from their gestures and the expression in their eyes they seemed to feel as if God had sent them our succour.[129]

The retrospectively constructed image of the flogged, defeated Zulu—a dumb animal conveying his gratitude to God's missionaries of peace—is completely at odds, as we shall see, with his views about Zulus that were published in the pages of his newspapers during those years. In Gandhi's reimagining of the story of the Bambatha Rebellion, the broken Zulu becomes the inspiration for another of his causes: celibacy.

While I was working with the Corps, two ideas which had long been floating in my mind became firmly fixed. First, an aspirant after a life exclusively devoted to service must lead a life of celibacy. Second, he must accept poverty as a constant companion through life. He may not take up any occupation which would prevent him or make him shrink from undertaking the lowliest of duties or largest risks.[130]

Gandhi's experiments with poverty and celibacy began in the Phoenix Settlement, a commune he had set up in 1904. It was built on a hundred-acre plot of land in the heart of Natal amidst the sugar fields that were worked by Indian indentured labour. The members of the commune included a few Europeans and (non-indentured) Indians, but no Black Africans.

In September 1906, only months after the Bambatha Rebellion, despite his offers of friendship and his demonstrations of loyalty, Gandhi was let down once again. The British government passed the Transvaal Asiatic Law Amendment Act. Its purpose was to control Indian merchants (who were regarded as competition to White traders) from entering the Transvaal.[131] Every male Asian had to register himself and produce on demand a thumbprinted certificate of identity. Unregistered people were liable to be deported. There was no right of appeal. Suddenly, a community whose leader had been dreaming of an "Imperial Brotherhood" had been once again reduced "to a status lower than that of the aboriginal races of South Africa and the Coloured People".[132]

Gandhi led the struggle of the passenger Indians bravely, and from the front. Two thousand people burned their passes in a public bonfire; Gandhi was assaulted mercilessly, arrested and imprisoned. And then his worst nightmares became a reality. The man who could not bear to even share the entrance to a post office with 'Kaffirs' now had to share a prison cell with them:

> We were all prepared for hardships, but not quite for this experience. We could understand not being classed with the Whites, but to be placed on the same level with the Natives seemed to be too much to put up with. I then felt that Indians had not launched our passive resistance too soon. Here was further proof that the obnoxious law was meant to emasculate the Indians... Apart from whether or not this implies degradation, I must say it is rather dangerous. Kaffirs as a rule are uncivilised—the convicts even more so. They are troublesome, very dirty and live almost like animals.[133]

A year later, the sixteenth of the twenty years he would spend in South Africa, he wrote "My Second Experience in Gaol" in *Indian Opinion* (16 January 1909):

> I was given a bed in a cell where there were mostly Kaffir prisoners who had been lying ill. I spent the night in this cell in great misery and fear... I read the *Bhagvad Gita* which I had carried with me. I read the verses which had a bearing on my situation and meditating on them, managed to compose myself. The reason why I felt so uneasy was that the Kaffir and Chinese prisoners

appeared to be wild, murderous and given to immoral ways... He [the Chinese] appeared to be worse. He came near the bed and looked closely at me. I kept still. Then he went to a Kaffir lying in bed. The two exchanged obscene jokes, uncovering each other's genitals... I have resolved in my mind on an agitation to ensure that Indian prisoners are not lodged with Kaffirs or others. We cannot ignore the fact that there is no common ground between them and us. Moreover those who wish to sleep in the same room as them have ulterior motives for doing so.[134]

From inside jail Gandhi began to petition the White authorities for separate wards in prisons. He led battles demanding segregation on many counts: he wanted separate blankets because he worried that "a blanket that has been used by the dirtiest of Kaffirs may later fall to an Indian's lot".[135] He wanted prison meals specially suited to Indians—rice served with ghee[136]—and refused to eat the "mealie pap" that the 'Kaffirs' seemed to relish. He also agitated for separate lavatories for Indian prisoners.[137]

Twenty years later, in 1928, the 'Truth' about all this had transmogrified into another story altogether. Responding to a proposal for segregated education for Indians and Africans in South Africa, Gandhi wrote:

Indians have too much in common with the Africans to think of isolating themselves from them. They cannot exist in South Africa for any length of time without the active sympathy and friendship of the Africans. I am not aware of the general body of the Indians having ever adopted an air of superiority towards their African brethren, and it would be a tragedy if any such movement were to gain ground among the Indian settlers of South Africa.[138]

Then, in 1939, disagreeing with Jawaharlal Nehru, who believed that Black Africans and Indians should stand together against the White regime in South Africa, Gandhi contradicted himself once more: "However much one may sympathise with the Bantus, Indians cannot make common cause with them."[139]

Gandhi was an educated, well-travelled man. He would have been aware of the winds that were blowing in other parts of the world. His disgraceful words about Africans were written around the same time W.E.B. Du Bois wrote *The Souls of Black Folk*: "One ever feels this two-ness—an American, a Negro; two souls, two thoughts, two un-reconciled strivings; two warring ideals in one dark body, whose dogged strength alone keeps it from being torn asunder."[140]

Gandhi's attempts to collaborate with a colonial regime were taking place at the same time that the anarchist Emma Goldman was saying:

> The centralisation of power has brought into being an international feeling of solidarity among the oppressed nations of the world; a solidarity which represents a greater harmony of interests between the working man of America and his brothers abroad than between the American miner and his exploiting compatriot; a solidarity which fears not foreign invasion, because it is bringing all the workers to the point when they will say to their masters, 'Go and do your own killing. We have done it long enough for you.'[141]

Pandita Ramabai (1858–1922), Gandhi's contemporary from India, did not have his unfortunate instincts. Though she was born a Brahmin, she renounced Hinduism for its patriarchy and its practice of caste, became a Christian, and quarrelled with the Anglican Church too, earning a place of pride in India's anticaste tradition. She travelled to the US in 1886 where she met Harriet Tubman, who had once been a slave, whom she admired more than anybody she had ever met. Contrast Gandhi's attitude towards the African people to Pandita Ramabai's description of her meeting with Harriet Tubman:

> Harriet still works. She has a little house of her own, where she and her husband live and work together for their own people... Harriet is very large and strong. She hugged me like a bear and shook me by the hand till my poor little hand ached![142]

In 1873, Jotiba Phule dedicated his *Gulamgiri* (Slavery) to

> The good people of the United States as a token of admiration
> for their sublime disinterested and self sacrificing devotion in
> the cause of Negro Slavery; and with an earnest desire, that my
> countrymen may take their noble example as their guide in the
> emancipation of their Shudra Brothers from the trammels of
> Brahmin thraldom.[143]

Phule—who, among other things, campaigned for
widow remarriage, girls' education, and started a school for
Untouchables—described how "the owners of slaves treated the
slaves as beasts of burden, raining kicks and blows on them all
the time and starving them", and how they would "harness the
slaves as bullocks and make them plough the fields in the blazing
sun". Phule believed that the Shudra and Ati-Shudra would
understand slavery better than anyone else because "they have
a direct experience of slavery as compared to the others who
have never experienced it so; the Shudras were conquered and
enslaved by the Brahmins".[144]

The connection between racism and casteism was made more
than a century before the 2001 Durban conference. Empathy
sometimes achieves what scholarship cannot.

▼

Despite all of Gandhi's suffering in unsegregated South African
prisons, the satyagraha against the Pass Laws did not gain much
traction. After leading a number of protests against registering
and fingerprinting, Gandhi suddenly announced that Indians
would agree to be fingerprinted as long as it was voluntary.
It would not be the first time that he would make a deal that
contradicted what the struggle was about in the first place.

Around this time, his wealthy architect friend Hermann

Kallenbach gifted him 1,100 acres of farmland just outside Johannesburg. Here he set up his second commune, Tolstoy Farm, with one thousand fruit trees on it. On Tolstoy Farm he began his experiments in purity and spirituality, and developed his home-grown protocol for the practice of satyagraha. Given Gandhi's proposals to partner with the British in their colonisation of South Africa—and British reluctance to accept that partnership—satyagraha, appealing to your opponent with the force of Truth and Love, was the perfect political tool. Gandhi was not trying to overwhelm or destroy a ruling structure; he simply wanted to be friends with it. The intensity of his distaste for the "raw Kaffir" was matched by his affection and admiration for the British. Satyagraha seemed to be a way of reassuring them, a way of saying: "You can trust us. Look at us. We would rather harm ourselves than harm you". (This is not to suggest that satyagraha is not, and cannot be, in certain situations, an effective means of political resistance. I am merely describing the circumstances in which Gandhi began his experiments with satyagraha.)

Essentially, his idea of satyagraha revolved around a regimen of renunciation and purification. Renunciation naturally segued into a missionary approach to politics. The emphasis on purity and purification obviously derived from the caste system, though Gandhi inverted the goalposts and called his later ministrations to Untouchables a process of 'self-purification'. On the whole, it was a brand of hair-shirt Christianity combined with his own version of Hinduism and esoteric vegetarianism (which ended up underlining the 'impurity' of Dalits, Muslims and all the rest of us meat-eaters—in other words, the majority of the Indian population). The other attraction was *brahmacharya*—celibacy. The practice of semen retention and complete sexual abstinence became the minimum qualification for a 'pure' satyagrahi. Crucifixion of the flesh, denial of pleasure and desire—and eventually almost every normal human instinct—became a major theme. Even eating came in for some serious stick: "Taking food is as dirty an act as answering the call of nature".[145]

Would a person who was starving think of eating as a 'dirty act'?

Gandhi always said that he wanted to live like the poorest of the poor. The question is, can poverty be simulated? Poverty, after all, is not just a question of having no money or no possessions. Poverty is about having no power. As a politician, it was Gandhi's business to accumulate power, which he did effectively. Satyagraha wouldn't have worked, even as much as it did, if it wasn't for his star power. If you are powerful, you can live simply, but you cannot be poor. In South Africa, it took a lot of farmland and organic fruit trees to keep Gandhi in poverty.

The battle of the poor and the powerless is one of reclamation, not renunciation. But Gandhi, like many successful godmen, was an astute politician. He understood that the act of renunciation by someone who has plenty to renounce has always appealed to the popular imagination. (Gandhi would eventually discard his Western suit and put on a dhoti in order to dress like the poorest of the poor. Ambedkar, on the other hand, born unmoneyed, Untouchable, and denied the right to wear clothes that privileged-caste people wore, would show his defiance by wearing a three-piece suit.)

The irony is that while Gandhi was performing the rituals of poverty in Tolstoy Farm, he was not questioning the accumulation of capital or the unequal distribution of wealth. He was not holding out for improved working conditions for the indentured, or for the return of land to those it had been stolen from. He was fighting for Indian merchants' right to expand their businesses to the Transvaal and to compete with British merchants.

For centuries before Gandhi and for years after him, Hindu rishis and yogis have practised feats of renunciation far more arduous than Gandhi's. However, they have usually done it alone, on a snowy mountainside or in a cave set in a windblown cliff. Gandhi's genius was that he yoked his other-worldly search for *moksha* to a very worldly, political cause and performed both, like a fusion dance, for a live audience, in a live-in theatre. Over the years, he expanded his strange experiments to include his wife as well as other people, some of them too young to know what they were being subjected to. Towards the end of his life, as an old man in his seventies, he took to sleeping with two young girls, Manu, his seventeen-year-old grand-niece, and Abha (who were known as his "walking sticks").[146] He did this, he said, in order to gauge the degree of success or failure of his conquest over sexual desire. Leaving aside the very contentious, disturbing issues of consent and propriety, leaving aside the effect it had on the girls, the 'experiment' raises another distressing, almost horrifying question. For Gandhi to extrapolate from the 'results' of sleeping with two (or three, or four) women that he had, or had not, conquered heterosexual desire suggests that he viewed women not as individuals, but as a category. That, for him, a very small sample of a few physical specimens, including his own grand-niece, could stand in for the whole species.

Gandhi wrote at length about the experiments he conducted at Tolstoy Farm. On one occasion, he describes how he slept with young boys and girls spread around him, "taking care to arrange the order of the beds", but knowing full well that "any amount of such care would have been futile in case of a wicked mind". Then:

> I sent the boys reputed to be mischievous and the innocent young girls to bathe in the same spot at the same time. I had fully explained the duty of self-restraint to the children, who were all familiar with my Satyagraha doctrine. I knew, and so did the children, that I loved them with a mother's love... Was it a folly to let the children meet there for bath and yet to expect them to

be innocent?

The 'trouble' that Gandhi had been anticipating—spoiling for, actually—with a mother's prescience, took place:

> One day, one of the young men made fun of two girls, and the girls themselves or some child brought me the information. The news made me tremble. I made inquiries and found that the report was true. I remonstrated with the young men, but that was not enough. I wished the two girls to have some sign on their person as a warning to every young man that no evil eye might be cast upon them, and as a lesson to every girl that no one dare assail their purity. The passionate Ravana could not so much as touch Sita with evil intent while Rama was thousands of miles away. What mark should the girls bear so as to give them a sense of security and at the same time to sterilise the sinner's eye? This question kept me awake for the night.

By morning, Gandhi had made his decision. He "gently suggested to the girls that they might let him cut off their fine long hair". At first they were reluctant. He kept the pressure up and managed to win the elderly women of the farm over to his side. The girls came around after all, "and at once the very hand that is narrating this incident set to cut off their hair. And afterwards analysed and explained my procedure before my class, with excellent results. I never heard of a joke again".[147]

There is no mention of what punishment the same mind that had thought up the idea of cutting the girls' hair had thought up for the boys.

Gandhi did indeed make the space for women to participate in the national movement. But those women had to be virtuous; they had to, so to speak, bear "marks" upon their person that would "sterilise the sinner's eye". They had to be obedient women who never challenged the traditional structures of patriarchy.

Gandhi may have enjoyed and learned a great deal from his

'experiments'. But he's gone now, and left his followers with a legacy of a joyless, joke-free world: no desire, no sex—which he described as a poison worse than snakebite[148]—no food, no beads, no nice clothes, no dance, no poetry. And very little music. It is true that Gandhi fired the imagination of millions of people. It's also true that he has debilitated the political imagination of millions with his impossible standards of 'purity' and righteousness as a minimum qualification for political engagement:

> Chastity is one of the greatest disciplines without which the mind cannot attain the requisite firmness. A man who loses stamina becomes emasculated and cowardly... Several questions arise: How is one to carry one's wife with one? Yet those who wish to take part in great work are bound to solve these puzzles.[149]

No questions seem to have arisen as to how one was to carry one's *husband* with one. Nor any thoughts on whether satyagraha would be effective, for example, against the hoary tradition of marital rape.

▼

In 1909, Gandhi published his first and most famous political tract, *Hind Swaraj*. It was written in Gujarati and translated into English by Gandhi himself. It is considered to be a piece of genuinely original thinking, a classic. Gandhi himself remained pleased with it to the end of his days. *Hind Swaraj* defines Gandhi in the way *Annihilation of Caste* defines Ambedkar. Soon after it was published, copies of it were seized in Bombay, and it was banned for being seditious. The ban was lifted only in 1938.[150]

It was conceived of as Gandhi's response to Indian socialists, impatient young nihilists and nationalists he had met in London. Like the *Bhagvad Gita* (and Jotiba Phule's *Gulamgiri*), *Hind Swaraj* is written as a conversation between two people. Its best and most grounded passages are those in which he writes about how Hindus and Muslims would have to learn to accommodate each other after swaraj. This message of tolerance and inclusiveness between Hindus and Muslims continues to be Gandhi's real, lasting and most important contribution to the idea of India.

Nevertheless, in *Hind Swaraj*, Gandhi (like many right-wing Hindu nationalists would do in the future)[151] superimposes Hinduism's spiritual map—the map of its holy places—on the territorial map of India, and uses that to define the boundaries of the country. By doing so, consciously or unconsciously, Gandhi presents the Homeland as unmistakably Hindu. But he goes on, in the manner of a good host, to say that "a country must have a faculty for assimilation" and that "the Hindus, the Mohammedans, the Parsees and the Christians who have made India their country, are fellow countrymen".[152] The time Gandhi spent in South Africa—where the majority of his clients, and later his political constituency, were wealthy Muslim businessmen—seems to have made him more attentive to the Muslim question than he might have otherwise been. For the sin of this attentiveness, this obviously unforgivable complexity, he paid with his life.

The rest of *Hind Swaraj* is a trenchant (some say lyrical) denunciation of modernity. Like the Luddites, but with no calls for machine smashing, it indicts the industrial revolution and modern machinery. It calls the British Parliament a "sterile woman" and a "prostitute". It condemns doctors, lawyers and the railways, and dismisses Western civilisation as "satanic". It might not have been a crude or even excessive adjective to use from the point of view of the genocide of tens of millions of people in the Americas, in Australia, the Congo and West Africa that was an inalienable part of the colonial project. But it was a little odd, considering Gandhi's proposals for an "Imperial

Brotherhood". And even odder, considering his respect for the British and his disdain for the uncivilised "raw Kaffir". "What then is civilisation?" the 'Reader' eventually asks the 'Editor'. The Editor then launches into an embarrassing, chauvinistic reverie of a mythical India: "I believe that the civilisation India has evolved is not to be beaten in the world".[153] It's tempting to reproduce the whole chapter, but since that isn't possible, here are some key passages:

> A man is not necessarily happy because he is rich or unhappy because he is poor. The rich are often seen to be unhappy, the poor to be happy. Millions will always remain poor... Observing all this our ancestors dissuaded us from luxuries and pleasures. We have managed with the same kind of plough as it existed thousands of years ago. We have retained the same kind of cottages we had in former times and our indigenous education remains the same as before. We have had no system of life-corroding competition. Each followed his own occupation or trade. And charged a regulation wage. It was not that we did not know how to invent machinery, but our forefathers knew that, if we set our hearts after such things we would become slaves and lose our moral fibre... A nation with a constitution like this is fitter to teach others than to learn from others. This nation had courts, lawyers and doctors, but they were all within bounds... Justice was tolerably fair.[154]

Gandhi's valorisation of the mythic village came at a point in his life when he does not seem to have even visited an Indian village.[155] And yet his faith in it is free of doubt or caveats.

> The common people lived independently, and followed their agricultural occupation. They enjoyed true Home Rule. And where this cursed modern civilisation has not reached, India remains as it was before... I would certainly advise you and those like you who love the motherland to go into the interior that has yet not been polluted by the railways, and to live there for at least six months; you might be patriotic and speak of Home Rule.

Now you see what I consider to be real civilisation. Those who want to change conditions such as I have described are enemies of the country and are sinners.[156]

Other than the vague allusion to the idea of people following an ancestral occupation or trade that was rewarded by a "regulation wage", caste is absent in Gandhi's reverie. Though Gandhi later insisted that untouchability had troubled him since he was a boy,[157] in *Hind Swaraj* he makes absolutely no mention of it.

Around the time *Hind Swaraj* was published, the first biographies of Gandhi were also published: *M.K. Gandhi: An Indian Patriot in South Africa* by Reverend Joseph Doke (a minister of the Johannesburg Baptist Church) in 1909, and *M.K. Gandhi: A Sketch of His Life and Work* in 1910 by Henry S.L. Polak, one of Gandhi's closest friends and most admiring of disciples. These contained the first intimations of coming Mahatmahood.

In 1910, the separate British colonies of Natal, the Cape, the Transvaal and the Orange Free State united to become the Union of South Africa, a self-governing Dominion under the British crown, with Louis Botha as its first Prime Minister. Segregation began to harden.

Around then, only three years before he was to leave South Africa, Gandhi condescendingly began to admit that Africans were the original inhabitants of the land:

The negroes alone are the original inhabitants of this land. We have not seized the land from them by force; we live here with their goodwill. The whites, on the other hand, have occupied the country forcibly and appropriated it to themselves.[158]

By now he seems to have forgotten that he had actively collaborated with the Whites in their wars to forcibly occupy the country, appropriate the land and enslave Africans. Gandhi chose to ignore the scale and extent of the brutality that was taking place around him. Did he really believe that it was the "negroes' goodwill" that allowed Indian merchants to ply their trade in South Africa, and not, despite its racist laws, British colonialism? In 1906, during the Zulu rebellion, he had been less woolly about things like "goodwill" when he said, "We are in Natal by virtue of British Power. Our very existence depends on it".

By 1911, the anxiety of the White folks about the burgeoning Indian population led to legislation that stopped the import of labour from India.[159] Then came 1913—the year the first volume of Marcel Proust's À la recherche du temps perdu was first published, the year Rabindranath Tagore won the Nobel Prize for literature—South Africa's year of blood. It was the year the foundations for apartheid were laid, the year of the Land Act, legislation that created a system of tenure that deprived the majority of South Africa's inhabitants of the right to own land. It was the year African women marched against the Pass Laws that herded them into townships and restricted inter-province movement, the year White mine workers and railway workers, and then African mine workers, went on strike. It was the year Indian workers rose against a new three-pound tax and against a new marriage law that made their existing marriages illegal and their children illegitimate. The year the three-pound tax was imposed on those who had worked off their indenture and wanted to live on in South Africa as free citizens. Being unaffordable, the tax would have forced workers to re-indenture and lock themselves into a cycle of servitude.

For the first time in twenty years, Gandhi aligned himself politically with the people he had previously taken care to distance himself from. He stepped in to 'lead' the Indian workers' strike. In fact, they did not need 'leading'. For years before, during and after Gandhi, they had waged their own heroic resistance. It could be argued that they were fortunate to have escaped Gandhi's attentions, because they did not just wage a resistance, they also broke caste in the only way it can be broken—they transgressed caste barriers, got married to each other, made love and had babies.

Gandhi travelled from town to town, addressing coal miners and plantation workers. The strike spread from the collieries to the sugar plantations. Non-violent satyagraha failed. There was rioting, arson and bloodshed. Thousands were arrested as they defied the new immigration bill and crossed the border into the Transvaal. Gandhi was arrested too. He lost control of the strike. Eventually, he signed a settlement with Jan Smuts. The settlement upset many in the Indian community, who saw it as a pyrrhic victory. One of its most controversial clauses was the one in which the government undertook to provide free passage to Indians who wished to return permanently to India. It reinforced and formalised the idea that Indians were sojourners who could be repatriated. (In their 1948 election manifesto the apartheid National Party called for the repatriation of all Indians. Indians finally became full-fledged citizens only in 1960, when South Africa became a republic.)

P.S. Aiyar, an old adversary of Gandhi's, had accused him of being primarily concerned with the rights of the passenger Indians. (During the struggle against the first proposal of the draft Immigration Bill in 1911, while some Indians, including Aiyar, were agitating for the free movement of all Indians to all provinces, Gandhi and Henry Polak were petitioning for six new entrants a year to be allowed into the Transvaal.)[160] Aiyar was editor of the *African Chronicle*, a newspaper with a predominantly Tamil readership that reported the terrible conditions in which indentured labourers worked and lived. About the Gandhi–Smuts settlement, Aiyar said that Gandhi's "ephemeral fame and popularity in India rest on no glorious achievement for his countrymen, but on a series of failures, which has resulted in causing endless misery, loss of wealth, and deprivation of existing rights". He added that

Gandhi's leadership over the previous two decades had "resulted in no tangible good to anyone". On the contrary, Gandhi and his band of passive resisters had made themselves "an object of ridicule and hatred among all sections of the community in South Africa".[161] (A joke among some Blacks and Indians goes like this: Things were good then, back in 1893. Gandhi only got thrown *off* a train. By 1920, we couldn't even get *on* one.[162])

Though it was not put down in writing, part of the Gandhi–Smuts settlement seems to have been that Gandhi would have to leave South Africa.[163]

In all his years in South Africa, Gandhi maintained that Indians deserved better treatment than Africans. The jury is still out on whether or not Gandhi's political activity helped or harmed the Indian community in the long run. But his consistent attempts to collaborate with the British government certainly made the Indian community vulnerable during the rise of African nationalism. When Indian political activists joined the liberation movement under African leadership in the 1950s and saw their freedom as being linked to the freedom of African people, they were breaking with Gandhi's politics, not carrying on his legacy. When Indians joined the Black Consciousness Movement in the 1970s seeking to build a broader Black identity, they were actually upending Gandhian politics. It is these people, many of whom did their time in Robben Island with Nelson Mandela and other African comrades, who have saved the South African Indian community from being painted as a race of collaborators and from being isolated, even expelled, like the Indians in Uganda were in 1972.

That Gandhi is a hero in South Africa is as undeniable as it is baffling. One possible explanation is that after he left South Africa, Gandhi was *reimported*, this time as the shining star of the freedom struggle in India. The Indian community in South Africa, already cut adrift from its roots, was, after Gandhi left, further isolated and brutalised by the apartheid regime. Gandhi's cult status in India and his connection to South Africa would have provided South African Indians with a link to their history and their motherland.

In order for Gandhi to be a South African hero, it became necessary to rescue him from his past, and rewrite it. Gandhi himself began that project. Some writers of history completed it. Towards the end of Gandhi's stay in South Africa, the first few biographies had spread the news, and things were moving fast on the messiah front. The young Reverend Charles Freer Andrews travelled to South Africa and fell on his knees when he met Gandhi at the Durban dock.[164] Andrews, who became a lifelong devotee, went on to suggest that Gandhi, the leader of the "humblest, the lowliest and lost", was a living avatar of Christ's spirit. Europeans and Americans vied with each other to honour him.

In 1915, Gandhi returned to India via London where he was awarded something far better than the Queen's chocolate. For his services to the British Empire, he was honoured with the Kaisar-i-Hind Gold Medal for Public Service, presented to him by Lord Hardinge of Penshurst. (He returned it in 1920 before the first national Non-Cooperation Movement.) Honoured thus, he arrived in India fitted out as the Mahatma—Great Soul—who had fought racism and imperialism and had stood up for the rights of Indian workers in South Africa. He was forty-six years old.

To honour the returning hero, G.D. Birla, a leading Indian industrialist (and a fellow Bania), organised a grand reception in Calcutta. The Birlas ran an export–import business based in Calcutta and Bombay. They traded in cotton, wheat and silver. G.D. Birla was a wealthy man who was chafing at the bit, offended by the racism he had personally encountered at the hands of the British. He had had several run-ins with the colonial government. He became Gandhi's chief patron and sponsor and paid him a generous monthly retainer to cover the costs of running his ashrams and for his Congress party work. There were other industrialist sponsors as well, but Gandhi's arrangement with G.D. Birla lasted for the rest of his days.[165] In addition to mills and other businesses, G.D. Birla owned a newspaper, *Hindustan Times*, where Gandhi's son, Devdas, eventually worked as managing editor.

So the Mahatma who promoted homespun khadi and the wooden charkha was sponsored by a mill-owner. The man who raged against the machine was kept afloat by industrialists. This arrangement was the precursor to the phenomenon of the corporate-sponsored NGO.

Once the finances were in place and the ashrams were up and running, Gandhi set off on his mission of rallying people against the British government, yet never harming the old hierarchies that he (and his sponsors) intrinsically believed in. He travelled the length and breadth of the country to get to know it. His first satyagraha was in Champaran, Bihar, in 1917. Three years prior to his arrival there, landless peasants living on the verge of famine, labouring on British-owned indigo plantations, had risen in revolt against a new regime of British taxes. Gandhi travelled to Champaran and set up an ashram from where he backed their struggle. The people were not sure exactly who he was. Jacques Pouchepadass, who studied the Champaran Satyagraha, writes: "Rumours ... reported that Gandhi had been sent into Champaran by the Viceroy, or even the King, to redress all the grievances of the raiyats [farmers] and that his mandate overruled all the local officials and the courts."[166] Gandhi stayed in Champaran for a year and then left. Says Pouchepadass, "It is a fact that from 1918 onwards, after Gandhi had left and the planters' influence had begun to fade away, the hold of the rural oligarchy grew stronger than ever".

To rouse people against injustice and yet control them and persuade them to *his* view of injustice, Gandhi had to make some complicated manoeuvres. In 1921, when peasants (kisans) rose against their Indian landlords (zamindars) in the United Provinces, Gandhi sent them a message:

> Whilst we will not hesitate to advise kisans when the moment comes to suspend payment of taxes to Government, it is not contemplated that at any stage of non-cooperation we would seek to deprive the zamindars of their rent. The kisan movement must be confined to the improvement of the status of the kisans and the betterment of the relations between the zamindars and them. The kisans must be advised scrupulously to abide by the terms of their agreement with the zamindars, whether such agreement is written or inferred from custom.[167]

Inferred from custom. We needn't guess what that means. It's the whole ball of wax.

Though Gandhi spoke of inequality and poverty, though he sometimes even sounded like a socialist, at no point in his political career did he ever seriously criticise or confront an Indian industrialist or the landed aristocracy. This was of a piece with his doctrine of trusteeship or what today goes by the term Corporate Social Responsibility (CSR). Expanding on this in an essay called "Equal Distribution", Gandhi said: "The rich man will be left in possession of his wealth, of which he will use what he reasonably requires for his personal needs and will act as a trustee for the remainder to be used for society. In this argument, honesty on the part of the trustee is assumed".[168] To justify the idea of the rich becoming the "guardians of the poor", he argued that "the rich cannot accumulate wealth without the co-operation of the poor in society".[169] And then, to empower the poor wards of the rich guardians: "If this knowledge were to penetrate to and spread amongst the poor, they would become strong and would learn how to free themselves by means of non-violence from the crushing inequalities which have brought them to the verge of starvation".[170] Gandhi's ideas of trusteeship echo almost verbatim what American capitalists—the Robber Barons—like J.D. Rockefeller and Andrew Carnegie were saying at the time. Carnegie writes in *The Gospel of Wealth* (1889):

> This, then, is held to be the duty of the man of Wealth: First, to set an example of modest, unostentatious living, shunning display or extravagance; to provide moderately for the legitimate wants of those dependent upon him; and after doing so to consider all surplus revenues which come to him simply as trust funds, which he is called upon to administer, and strictly bound as a matter of duty to administer, in the manner which, in his judgement, is best calculated to produce the most beneficial results for the community—the man of wealth thus becoming the mere agent and trustee for his poorer brethren, bringing to their service his superior wisdom, experience and ability to administer, doing for them better than they would or could do for themselves.[171]

The contradictions mattered little, because by then, Gandhi was far beyond all that. He was a Sanatani Hindu (which is how he described himself), and an avatar of Christ (which is how he allowed himself to be described). The trains he travelled in were mobbed by devotees seeking 'darshan' (a sighting). The biographer D.G. Tendulkar, who travelled with him, describes the phenomenon as "mass conversions to the new creed".

> This simple faith moved India's millions who greeted him everywhere with cries of 'Mahatma Gandhi ki Jai'. Prostitutes of Barisal, the Marwari merchants of Calcutta, Oriya coolies, railway strikers, Santhals eager to present khadi chaadars, all claimed his attention ... wherever he went he had to endure the tyranny of love.[172]

In his classic essay, "Gandhi as Mahatma", the historian Shahid Amin describes how the combination of cleverly planted rumours by local Congress leaders, adulatory—and sometimes hallucinatory—newspaper reporting, a gullible people and Gandhi's extraordinary charisma built up mass hysteria which culminated in the deification of Mahatma Gandhi. Even back then, not everyone was convinced. An editorial in *The Pioneer* of 23 April 1921 said, "The very simple people in the east and south of the United Provinces afford a fertile soil in which a belief in the power of the 'mahatmaji', who is after all little more than a name of power to them, may grow." The editorial was criticising an article that had appeared in *Swadesh*, a Gorakhpur newspaper, that had published rumours about the miracles that surrounded Gandhi: he had made fragrant smoke waft up from a well, a copy of the Holy Quran had appeared in a locked room, a buffalo that belonged to an Ahir who refused money to a sadhu begging in the Mahatma's name had perished in a fire, and a Brahmin who had defied Gandhi's authority had gone mad.[173]

The taproot of Gandhi's Mahatmahood had found its way into a fecund rill, where feudalism met the future, where miracles met modernity. From there it drew sustenance and prospered.

The sceptics were few and did not count for much. Gandhi was by now addressing rallies of up to two hundred thousand people. The hysteria spread abroad. In 1921, the Unitarian minister John Haynes Holmes of the Community Church in New York in a sermon called "Who is the Greatest Man in the World?" introduced Gandhi to his congregation as "The Suffering Christ of the twentieth century".[174] Years later, in 1958, Martin Luther King, Jr would do the same: "Christ furnished the spirit and motivation, while Gandhi furnished the method."[175] They presented Gandhi with a whole new constituency: a paradoxical gift for a man who so feared and despised Africans.

Perhaps because the Western Christian world was apprehensive about the spreading influence of the Russian Revolution, and was traumatised by the horror of the First World War, Europeans and Americans vied to honour the living avatar of Christ. It didn't seem to matter that unlike Gandhi, who was from a well-to-do family (his father was the prime minister of the princely state of Porbandar), Jesus was a carpenter from the slums of Jerusalem who stood up against the Roman Empire instead of trying to make friends with it. And he wasn't sponsored by big business.

The most influential of Gandhi's admirers was the French dramatist Romain Rolland, who won the Nobel Prize for literature in 1915. He had not met Gandhi when in 1924 he published *Mahatma Gandhi: The Man Who Became One with the Universal Being*. It sold more than a hundred thousand copies and was translated into several European languages.[176] It opens with Tagore's invocation from the Upanishads:

> He is the One Luminous, Creator of All, Mahatma,
> Always in the hearts of the people enshrined,
> Revealed through Love, Intuition and Thought,
> Whoever knows him, Immortal becomes

Gandhi said he found a "real vision of truth" in the book. He called Rolland his "self-chosen advertiser" in Europe.[177] By 1924, on the list of executives of his own organisation, All-India Spinners Association, his name appeared as Mahatma Gandhi.[178] Sad then, for him to say in the first paragraph of his response to *Annihilation of Caste*: "Whatever label he wears in the future, Dr Ambedkar is not the man to allow himself to be forgotten". As though pointing to the profound horrors of the caste system was just a form of self-promotion for Ambedkar.

This is the man, or, if you are so inclined, the Saint, that Doctor Bhimrao Ramji Ambedkar, born in 1891 into an Untouchable Mahar family, presumed to argue with.

THE CACTUS GROVE

Ambedkar's father Ramji Sakpal and both his grandfathers

were soldiers in the British Army. They were Mahars from the Konkan, then a part of the Bombay Presidency and, at the time, a hotbed of nationalist politics. The two famous Congressmen, Bal Gangadhar Tilak of the 'garam dal' (militant faction) and Gandhi's mentor, Gopal Krishna Gokhale, of the 'naram dal' (moderate faction), were both Chitpavan Brahmins from the Konkan. (It was Tilak who famously said, "Swaraj is my birthright, and I shall have it".)

The Konkan coast was also home to Ambedkar's political forebear, Jotiba Phule, who called himself Joti Mali, the Gardener. Phule was from Satara, the town where Ambedkar spent his early childhood. The Mahars were considered Untouchables and, though they were landless agricultural labourers, they were comparatively better off than the other Untouchable castes. In the seventeenth century, they served in the army of Shivaji, the Maratha king of western India. After Shivaji's death, they served the Peshwas, an oppressive Brahminical regime that treated them horribly. (It was the Peshwas who forced Mahars to hang pots around their necks and tie brooms to their hips.) Unwilling to enter into a 'trusteeship' of this sort, the Mahars shifted their loyalty to the British. In 1818, in the Battle of Koregaon, a small British regiment of Mahar soldiers defeated the massive army of the last Peshwa ruler, Bajirao II.[179] The British subsequently raised a Mahar Regiment, which is still part of the Indian Army.

Over time, a section of the Mahar population left their villages and moved to the city. They worked in the Bombay mills and as casual, unorganised labour in the city. The move widened their horizons and perhaps accounts for why the Mahars were politicised quicker than other Untouchable communities in the region.

Ambedkar was born on 14 April 1891 in the cantonment town of Mhow near Indore in Central India. He was the fourteenth and last child of Ramji Sakpal and Bhimabai

Murbadkar Sakpal. His mother died when he was two years old, the same year that his father retired from the army. The family was brought up in the Bhakti tradition of Kabir and Tukaram, but Ramji Sakpal also educated his children in the Hindu epics. As a young boy, Ambedkar was sceptical about the Ramayana and the Mahabharata, and their capricious lessons in morality. He was particularly distressed by the story of the killing and dismembering of the 'low-born' Karna. (Karna was born of Surya, the Sun God, and the unmarried Kunti. Abandoned by his mother, he was brought up by a lowly charioteer. Karna was killed while he was repairing his chariot wheel on the battlefield by his half-brother Arjun on the advice of Krishna.) Ambedkar argued with his father: "Krishna believed in fraud. His life is nothing but a series of frauds. Equal dislike I have for Rama".[180] Later, in a series of essays called *Riddles in Hinduism*, published posthumously, he would expand on the themes of what he saw as inexcusable misogyny in Rama's and Krishna's slippery ethics.[181]

Ambedkar's encounters with humiliation and injustice began from his early childhood. When Gandhi was serving in the South African War, Ambedkar was ten years old, living with his aunt and going to a local government school in Satara. Thanks to a new British legislation,[182] he was *allowed* to go to a Touchable school, but he was made to sit apart from his classmates, on a scrap of gunnysack, so that he would not pollute the classroom floor. He remained thirsty all day because he was not allowed to drink from the Touchables' tap. Satara's barbers would not cut his hair, not even the barbers who sheared goats and buffaloes. This cruelty continued in school after school. His older brothers were not allowed to learn Sanskrit because it was the language of the Vedas, and the colonisation of knowledge was a central tenet of the caste system. (If a Shudra listens intentionally to the Vedas, the *Gautama Dharma Sutra* says, his ears must be filled with molten tin or lac.) Much later, in the 1920s, Ambedkar studied

Sanskrit (and in the 1940s also studied Pali), and became familiar with Brahminical texts—and when he wrote *Annihilation of Caste*, he deployed this knowledge explosively.

Eventually, in 1897, the family moved to a chawl in Bombay. In 1907, Ambedkar matriculated, the only Untouchable student in Elphinstone High School. It was an exceptional achievement for a Mahar boy. Soon after, he was married to nine-year-old Ramabai (not to be confused with Pandita Ramabai) in a ceremony that took place in a shed built over a city drain. While he was doing his bachelor's degree at Elphinstone College, a well-wisher introduced him to Sayajirao Gaekwad, the progressive Maharaja of Baroda. The Maharaja gave him a scholarship of Rs 25 a month to complete his graduation. The Maharaja was one of a number of unusual, privileged-caste Hindu individuals who helped or allied with Ambedkar in times of adversity and in his political confrontations.

The times were turbulent. The Morley–Minto reforms, which advocated a separate electorate for Muslims, had been passed. Nationalists were infuriated and saw the reforms as a British ploy to undermine the unity of the growing national movement. Tilak was convicted of sedition and deported to Mandalay. In 1910, Vinayak Damodar Savarkar, a young follower of Tilak, was arrested for organising an armed revolt against the Morley–Minto reforms. (In prison Savarkar turned towards political Hinduism and in 1923 wrote *Hindutva: Who Is a Hindu?*)

When Ambedkar graduated, he became one of three students who was given a scholarship by Sayajirao Gaekwad to travel abroad to continue his studies. In 1913 (Gandhi's last year in South Africa), the boy who had to sit on a gunnysack on his classroom floor was admitted to Columbia University in New York. It was while he was there, under the tutelage of John Dewey (of 'Deweyan liberalism' fame), Edwin Seligman, James Shotwell,

James Harvey Robinson and A.A. Goldenweiser, that he wrote his original, path-breaking paper on caste, "Castes in India: Their Mechanism, Genesis and Development",[183] in which he argued that caste could not be equated with either race or class, but was a unique social category in itself—an enclosed, endogamous class. When he wrote it, Ambedkar was only twenty-five years old. He returned briefly to India and then went to London to study economics at the London School of Economics and simultaneously take a degree in law at Gray's Inn in London—a degree he had to abandon halfway, but completed later.

Ambedkar returned to Baroda in 1917. To repay his scholarship, he was expected to serve as military secretary to the Maharaja. He came back to a very different reception from the one Gandhi received. There were no glittering ceremonies, no wealthy sponsors. On the contrary, from spending hours reading in the university library with its endless books, and eating at dining tables with napkins and cutlery, Ambedkar returned to the thorny embrace of the caste system. Afraid of even accidentally touching Ambedkar, clerks and peons in his office would fling files at him. Carpets were rolled up when he walked in and out of office so that they would not be polluted by him. He found no accommodation in the city: his Hindu, Muslim and Christian friends, even those he had known at Columbia, turned him down. Eventually, by masquerading as a Parsi, he got a room at a Parsi inn. When the owners discovered he was an Untouchable, he was thrown onto the street by armed men. "I can even now vividly recall it and never recall it without tears in my eyes", Ambedkar wrote. "It was then for the first time I learnt that a person who is Untouchable to a Hindu is also Untouchable to a Parsi".[184]

Unable to find accommodation in Baroda, Ambedkar returned to Bombay, where, after initially teaching private tutorials, he got a job as a professor at Sydenham College.

In 1917, Hindu reformers were wooing Untouchables with an edge of desperation. The Congress had passed its resolution against untouchability. Both Gandhi and Tilak called untouchability a 'disease' that was antithetical to Hinduism. The first All-India Depressed Classes Conference was held in Bombay, presided over by Ambedkar's patron and mentor, Maharaja Sayajirao Gaekwad, and attended by several luminaries of the time, including Tilak. They passed the All-India Anti-Untouchability Manifesto, which was signed by all of them (except Tilak, who managed to find a way around it).[185]

Ambedkar stayed away from these meetings. He had begun to grow sceptical about these very public but completely out-of-character displays of solicitude for Untouchables. He saw that these were ways in which, in the changing times, the privileged castes were manoeuvring to consolidate their control over the Untouchable community. While his audience, his constituency and his chief concern were the Untouchables, Ambedkar believed that it was not just the stigma, the pollution–purity issues around untouchability, but caste itself that had to be dismantled. The practice of untouchability, cruel as it was—the broom tied to the waist, the pot hung around the neck—was the performative, ritualistic end of the practice of caste. The real violence of caste was the denial of *entitlement*: to land, to wealth, to knowledge, to equal opportunity. (The caste system is the feudal version of the doctrine of trusteeship: the entitled must be left in possession of their entitlement, and be trusted to use it for the public good.)

How can a system of such immutable hierarchy be maintained if not by the threat of egregious, ubiquitous violence? How do landlords force labourers, generation after generation, to toil night and day on subsistence wages? Why would an Untouchable labourer, who is not allowed to even dream of being a landowner one day, put his or her life at the landlord's disposal, to plough the land, to sow seed and harvest the crop, if it were not out of sheer terror of the punishment that awaits the wayward? (Farmers, unlike industrialists, cannot afford strikes. Seed must be sown when it must be sown, the crop must be harvested when it must be harvested. The farmworker must be terrorised into abject submission, into being available when he must be available.) How were African slaves forced to work on American cotton fields? By being flogged, by being lynched, and if that did not work, by being hung from a tree for others to see and be afraid. Why are the murders of insubordinate Dalits even today never simply murders but ritual slaughter? Why are they always burnt alive, raped, dismembered and paraded naked? Why did Surekha Bhotmange and her children have to die the way they did?

Ambedkar tried to provide an answer:

> Why have the mass of people tolerated the social evils to which they have been subjected? There have been social revolutions in other countries of the world. Why have there not been social revolutions in India, is a question that has incessantly troubled me. There is only one answer which I can give and it is that the lower classes of Hindus have been completely disabled for direct action on account of this wretched caste system. They could not bear arms, and without arms they could not rebel. They were all ploughmen—or rather condemned to be ploughmen—and they were never allowed to convert their ploughshares into swords. They had no bayonets, and therefore everyone who chose, could and did sit upon them. On account of the caste system, they could receive no education. They could not think out or know the way to their salvation. They were condemned to be lowly; and not knowing the way of escape, and not having the means of escape, they became reconciled to eternal servitude, which they accepted as their inescapable fate.[186]

In rural areas, the threat of actual physical violence sometimes paled before the spectre of the 'social boycott' that orthodox Hindus would proclaim against any Untouchable who dared to defy the system. (This could mean anything from daring to buy a piece of land, wearing nice clothes, smoking a bidi in the presence of a caste Hindu, or having the temerity to wear shoes, or ride a mare in a wedding procession. The crime could even be an attitude, a posture that was less craven than an Untouchable's is meant to be.) It's the opposite of the boycott that the Civil Rights Movement in the US used as a campaign tool; the American Blacks at least had a modicum of economic clout to boycott buses and businesses that held them in contempt. Among privileged castes, the social boycott in rural India traditionally means 'hukka-pani bandh'—no hukka (tobacco) and no pani (water) for a person who has annoyed the community. Though it's called a 'social boycott', it is an *economic* as well as social boycott. For Dalits, that is lethal. The 'sinners' are denied employment in the neighbourhood, denied the right to food and water, denied the right to buy provisions in the village Bania's shop. They are hounded out and left to starve. The social boycott continues to be used as a weapon against Dalits in Indian villages. It is non-cooperation by the powerful against the powerless—non-cooperation, as we know it, turned on its head.

In order to detach caste from the political economy, from conditions of enslavement in which most Dalits lived and worked, in order to elide the questions of entitlement, land reforms and the redistribution of wealth, Hindu reformers cleverly narrowed the question of caste to the issue of untouchability. They framed it as an erroneous religious and cultural practice that needed to be reformed.

Gandhi narrowed it even further to the issue of 'Bhangis'—scavengers, a mostly urban and therefore somewhat politicised community. From his childhood, he resurrected the memory of Uka, the boy scavenger who used to service the household's lavatory, and often spoke of how the Gandhi family's treatment of Uka had always troubled him.[187] Rural Untouchables—ploughmen, potters, tanners and their families—lived in scattered, small communities, in hutments on the edges of villages (beyond polluting distance). Urban Untouchables—Bhangis, Chuhras and Mehtars—scavengers, as Gandhi liked to call them, lived together in numbers and actually formed a political constituency. In order to discourage them from converting to Christianity, Lala Mulk Raj Bhalla, a Hindu reformer of the Punjabi Khatri caste, re-baptised them in 1910, and they came to collectively be called Balmikis. Gandhi seized upon the Balmikis and made them his show window for untouchability. Upon them he performed his missionary acts of goodness and charity. He preached to them how to love and hold on to their heritage, and how to never aspire towards anything more than the joys of their hereditary occupation. All through his life, Gandhi wrote a great deal about the importance of 'scavenging' as a religious duty. It did not seem to matter that people in the rest of the world were dealing with their shit without making such a fuss about it.

Delivering the presidential address at the Kathiawar Political Conference in Bhavnagar on 8 January 1925, Gandhi said:

> If at all I seek any position it is that of a Bhangi. Cleansing of dirt is sacred work which can be done by a Brahmin as well as a Bhangi, the former doing it with and the latter without the knowledge of its holiness. I respect and honour both of them. In the absence of either of the two, Hinduism is bound to face extinction. I like the path of service; therefore, I like the Bhangi. I have personally no objection to sharing my meal with him, but I am not asking you to inter-dine with or inter-marry him. How can I advise you?[188]

Gandhi's attentiveness towards the Balmikis, his greatly publicised visits to 'Bhangi colonies', paid dividends, despite the fact that he treated them with condescension and contempt. When he stayed in one such colony in 1946:

half the residents were moved out before his visit and the shacks of the residents torn down and neat little huts constructed in their place. The entrances and windows of the huts were screened with matting, and during the length of Gandhi's visit, were kept sprinkled with water to provide a cooling effect. The local temple was white-washed and new brick paths were laid. In an interview with Margaret Bourke-White, a photo-journalist for *Life* magazine, one of the men in charge of Gandhi's visit, Dinanath Tiang of the Birla Company, explained the improvements in the untouchable colony, "We have cared for Gandhiji's comfort for the last twenty years".[189]

In his history of the Balmiki workers of Delhi, the scholar Vijay Prashad says when Gandhi staged his visits to the Balmiki Colony on Mandir Marg (formerly Reading Road) in 1946, he refused to eat with the community:

'You can offer me goat's milk', he said, 'but I will pay for it. If you are keen that I should take food prepared by you, you can come here and cook my food for me'... Balmiki elders recount tales of Gandhi's hypocrisy, but only with a sense of uneasiness. When a dalit gave Gandhi nuts, he fed them to his goat, saying that he would eat them later, in the goat's milk. Most of Gandhi's food, nuts and grains, came from Birla House; he did not take these from the dalits. Radical Balmikis took refuge in Ambedkarism which openly confronted Gandhi on these issues.[190]

Ambedkar realised that the problem of caste would only be further entrenched unless Untouchables were able to organise, mobilise and become a political constituency with their own representatives. He believed that reserved seats for Untouchables within the Hindu fold, or within the Congress, would just produce pliable candidates—servants who knew how to please their masters. He began to develop the idea of a separate electorate for Untouchables. In 1919, he submitted a written testimony to the Southborough Committee on electoral reforms.

The committee's brief was to propose a scheme of territorial constituencies based on existing land revenue districts, and separate communal representation for Muslims, Christians and Sikhs, for a new constitution that was to be drafted to prepare for Home Rule. The Congress boycotted the committee. To his critics, who called him a collaborator and a traitor, Ambedkar said that Home Rule was as much the right of the Untouchable as it was of the Brahmin, and it was the duty of privileged castes to do what they could to put everybody on an equal plane. In his testimony, Ambedkar argued that Untouchables were as separate a social group from Touchable Hindus as Muslims, Christians and Sikhs:

> The right of representation and the right to hold office under the State are the two most important rights that make up citizenship. But the untouchability of the untouchables puts these rights far beyond their reach. In a few places they do not even possess such insignificant rights as personal liberty and personal security, and equality before law is not always assured to them. These are the interests of the Untouchables. And as can be easily seen they can be represented by the Untouchables alone. They are distinctively their own interests and none else can truly voice them... Hence it is evident that we must find the Untouchables to represent their grievances which are their interests and, secondly, we must find them in such numbers as will constitute a force sufficient to claim redress.[191]

The British government did not, at that point, pay much attention to his testimony, though his presentation did perhaps provide the basis for Ambedkar being invited to the First Round Table Conference ten years later, in 1930.

Around this time, Ambedkar started his first journal, *Mook Nayak* (Leader of the Voiceless). Tilak's newspaper, *Kesari*, refused to carry even a paid advertisement announcing the publication of *Mook Nayak*.[192] The editor of *Mook Nayak* was P.N. Bhatkar, the first Mahar to matriculate and go to college.[193] Ambedkar wrote the first thirteen editorials himself. In the first one, he described Hindu society in a chilling metaphor—as a multi-storeyed tower with no staircase and no entrance. Everybody had to die in the storey they were born in.

In May 1920, backed by Chhatrapati Shahu, the Maharaja of Kolhapur, known for his anti-Brahmin views and for pioneering the policy of reservation in education and jobs as far back as 1902, Ambedkar and his colleagues organised the first All-India Depressed Classes Conference in Nagpur. It was agreed that no Untouchable representative chosen by a caste-Hindu majority could (or would) genuinely work against chaturvarna.

The 1920s marked the beginning of an era of direct action by Untouchables for the right to use wells, schools, courts, offices and public transport. In 1924, in what came to be known as the Vaikom Satyagraha, the Ezhavas, a community designated Shudra, and the Pulayas, who were Untouchables, agitated to use the public roads that skirted the Mahadeva temple in Vaikom, twenty miles from Kottayam in Travancore (now in the state of Kerala). One of the leaders of the Vaikom Satyagraha was George Joseph, a Syrian Christian, and an admirer of Gandhi. Gandhi, on his part, disapproved of a "non-Hindu" intervening in what he believed to be an "internal matter" of the Hindus.[194] (The same logic had not applied three years before, when he 'led' the Khilafat Movement.) He was also reluctant to support a full-blown satyagraha in an "Indian-ruled" state. During the course of the Vaikom Satyagraha, George Joseph was imprisoned. He became deeply disillusioned by what he saw as Gandhi's inexcusable ambivalence on the issue of caste. As the tension in Vaikom rose, C. Rajagopalachari,[195] Congress leader and Gandhi's chief lieutenant, travelled to Vaikom to oversee matters. On 27 May 1924, he reassured the worried privileged-caste Hindus of Vaikom in a public speech:

Let not the people of Vykom or any other place fear that
Mahatmaji wants caste abolished. Mahatmaji does not want the
caste system abolished but holds that untouchability should be
abolished... Mahatmaji does not want you to dine with Thiyas
or Pulayas. What he wants is that we must be prepared to touch
or go near other human beings as you go near a cow or a horse...
Mahatmaji wants you to look upon so-called untouchables as you
do at the cow and the dog and other harmless creatures.[196]

Gandhi himself arrived in Vaikom in March 1925 to arbitrate.
He consulted with the Brahmin priests of the temple—who did
not allow him, a non-Brahmin, to enter the sanctum—and the
Queen of Travancore, and negotiated a compromise: the roads
were realigned so that they were no longer within 'polluting'
distance from the temple. The contentious portion of the road
remained closed to Christians and Muslims as well as avarnas
(Untouchables) who continued to have no right to enter the
temple. Saying he was "unable to satisfy the orthodox friends"
Gandhi advised the "withdrawal of satyagraha",[197] but the local
satyagrahis continued with their struggle. Twelve years later,
in November 1936, the Maharaja of Travancore issued the first
Temple Entry Proclamation in India.[198]

▼

If one of Gandhi's first major political actions was the 'solution'
to the problem of the Durban Post Office, Ambedkar's was the
Mahad Satyagraha of 1927.

In 1923, the Legislative Council of Bombay (whose elections
had been boycotted by the Congress) passed a resolution, the
Bole Resolution, that allowed Untouchables to use public
tanks, wells, schools, courts and dispensaries. In the town of
Mahad, the municipality declared that it had no objection if
Untouchables used the Chavadar Tank in the town. Passing a

resolution was one thing, acting on it quite another. After four years of mobilisation, the Untouchables gathered courage and, in March 1927, held a two-day conference in Mahad. Money for the conference was raised by public contribution. In an unpublished manuscript, the scholar Anand Teltumbde quotes Anant Vinayak Chitre, one of the organisers of the Mahad Satyagraha, saying that forty villages contributed Rs 3 each, and a play about Tukaram was staged in Bombay that made Rs 23, making the total collection Rs 143. Contrast this with Gandhi's troubles. Just a few months before the Mahad Satyagraha, on 10 January 1927, Gandhi wrote to his industrialist-patron, G.D. Birla:

> My thirst for money is simply unquenchable. I need at least Rs 200,000—for Khadi, Untouchability and education. The dairy work makes another 50,000. Then there is the Ashram expenditure. No work remains unfinished for want of funds, but God gives after severe trials. This also satisfies me. You can give as you like for whatever work you have faith in.[199]

The Mahad conference was attended by about three thousand Untouchables, and a handful of progressive members of the privileged castes. (V.D. Savarkar, out of jail by now, was one of the supporters of the Mahad Satyagraha.) Ambedkar presided over the meeting. On the morning of the second day people decided to march to the Chavadar Tank and drink water. The privileged castes watched in horror as a procession of Untouchables walked through the town, four abreast, and drank water from the tank. After the shock subsided came the violent counter-attack, with clubs and sticks. Twenty Untouchables were injured. Ambedkar urged his people to stay firm and not to strike back. A rumour was deliberately spread that the Untouchables planned to enter the Veereshwar temple, which added a hysterical edge to the violence. The Untouchables scattered. Some found shelter in

Muslim homes. For his own safety, Ambedkar spent the night in the police station. Once calm returned, the Brahmins 'purified' the tank with prayers, and with 108 pots of cow dung, cow urine, milk, curd and ghee.[200] The symbolic exercise of their rights did not satisfy the Mahad satyagrahis. In June 1927, an advertisement appeared in *Bahishkrit Bharat* (Excluded India), a fortnightly Ambedkar had founded, asking those members of the Depressed Classes who wished to take the agitation further to enlist themselves. The orthodox Hindus of Mahad approached the sub-judge of the town and got a temporary legal injunction against the Untouchables using the tank. Still, the Untouchables decided to hold another conference and regrouped in Mahad in December. Ambedkar's disenchantment with Gandhi was still some years away. Gandhi had, in fact, spoken approvingly of the Untouchables' composure in the face of the attacks from the orthodoxy, so his portrait was put up on stage.[201]

Ten thousand people attended the second Mahad conference. On this occasion Ambedkar and his followers publicly burnt a copy of the *Manusmriti*,[202] and Ambedkar gave a stirring speech:

> Gentlemen, you have gathered here today in response to the invitation of the Satyagraha Committee. As the Chairman of that Committee, I gratefully welcome you all... This lake at Mahad is public property. The caste Hindus of Mahad are so reasonable that they not only draw water from the lake themselves but freely permit people of any religion to draw water from it, and accordingly people of other religions, such as Islam, do make use of this permission. Nor do the caste Hindus prevent members of species considered lower than the human, such as birds and beasts, from drinking at the lake. Moreover, they freely permit beasts kept by untouchables to drink at the lake.

> The caste Hindus of Mahad prevent the untouchables from drinking the water of the Chavadar Lake not because they suppose that the touch of the Untouchables will pollute the water

or that it will evaporate and vanish. Their reason for preventing
the Untouchables from drinking it is that they do not wish to
acknowledge by such permission that castes declared inferior by
sacred tradition are in fact their equals.

It is not as if drinking the water of the Chavadar Lake will make
us immortal. We have survived well enough all these days without
drinking it. We are not going to the Chavadar Lake merely to
drink its water. We are going to the Lake to assert that we too are
human beings like others. It must be clear that this meeting has
been called to set up the norm of equality...

Time and again Ambedkar returned to the theme of
equality. Men may not all be equal, he said, but equality was the
only possible governing principle because the classification and
assortment of human society was impossible.

To sum up, untouchability is not a simple matter; it is the mother
of all our poverty and lowliness and it has brought us to the abject
state we are in today. If we want to raise ourselves out of it, we must
undertake this task. We cannot be saved in any other way. It is a task
not for our benefit alone; it is also for the benefit of the nation.

Even this will not be enough. The inequality inherent in the four-
castes system must be rooted out... Our work has been begun to
bring about a real social revolution. Let no one deceive himself by
supposing that it is a diversion to quieten minds entranced with
sweet words. The work is sustained by strong feeling, which is the
power that drives the movement. No one can now arrest it. I pray
to god that the social revolution that begins here today may fulfil
itself by peaceful means. We say to our opponents too: please do not
oppose us. Put away the orthodox scriptures. Follow justice. And
we assure you that we shall carry out our programme peacefully.[203]

The thousands attending the conference were in a militant
mood, and wanted to defy the court injunction and march to
the tank. Ambedkar decided against it, hoping that after hearing
the matter, the courts would declare that Untouchables had the

right to use public wells. He thought that a judicial order would be a substantial step forward from just a municipal resolution. Although the High Court did eventually lift the injunction, it found a technical way around making a legal declaration in favour of the Untouchables.[204] (Like the judge who, almost eighty years later, wrote the Khairlanji verdict.)

That same month (December 1927), Gandhi spoke at the All-India Suppressed Classes Conference in Lahore, where he preached a gospel opposite to Ambedkar's. He urged Untouchables to fight for their rights by "sweet persuasion and not by Satyagraha which becomes Duragraha when it is intended to give rude shock to the deep-rooted prejudices of the people".[205] Duragraha, he defined as "devilish force", which was the polar opposite of Satyagraha, "soul force".[206]

Ambedkar never forgot Gandhi's response to the Mahad Satyagraha. Writing in 1945, in *What Congress and Gandhi Have Done to the Untouchables* he said:

> The Untouchables were not without hope of getting the moral support of Mr Gandhi. Indeed they had very good ground for getting it. For the weapon of satyagraha—the essence of which is to melt the heart of the opponent by suffering—was the weapon which was forged by Mr Gandhi, and who had led the Congress to practise it against the British Government for winning swaraj. Naturally the Untouchables expected full support from Mr Gandhi to their satyagraha against the Hindus the object of which was to establish their right to take water from public wells and to enter public Hindu temples. Mr Gandhi however did not give his support to the satyagraha. Not only did he not give his support, he condemned it in strong terms.[207]

▼

Logically, the direction in which Ambedkar was moving ought

to have made him a natural ally of the Communist Party of India, founded in 1925, two years before the Mahad Satyagraha. Bolshevism was in the air. The Russian Revolution had inspired communists around the world. In the Bombay Presidency, the trade union leader S.A. Dange, a Maharashtrian Brahmin, organised a large section of the Bombay textile workers into a breakaway union—India's first communist trade union—the Girni Kamgar Union, with seventy thousand members. At the time a large section of the workforce in the mills were Untouchables, many of them Mahars, who were employed only in the much lower-paid spinning department, because in the weaving department workers had to hold thread in their mouths, and the Untouchables' saliva was believed to be polluting to the product. In 1928, Dange led the Girni Kamgar Union's first major strike. Ambedkar suggested that one of the issues that ought to be raised was equality and equal entitlement *within* the ranks of workers. Dange did not agree, and this led to a long and bitter falling out.[208]

Years later, in 1949, Dange, who is still a revered figure in the communist pantheon, wrote a book, *Marxism and Ancient Indian Culture: India from Primitive Communism to Slavery*, in which he argued that ancient Hindu culture was a form of primitive communism in which "Brahman is the commune of Aryan man and yagnya [ritual fire sacrifice] is its means of production, the primitive commune with the collective mode of production". D.D. Kosambi, the mathematician and Marxist historian, said in a review: "This is so wildly improbable as to plunge into the ridiculous".[209]

The Bombay mills have since closed down, though the Girni Kamgar Union still exists. Mill workers are fighting for compensation and housing and resisting the takeover of mill lands for the construction of malls. The Communist Party has lost its influence, and the union has been taken over by the Shiv

Sena, a party of militant Maharashtrian Hindu chauvinists.

Years before Ambedkar and Dange were disagreeing about the internal inequalities between labourers, Gandhi was already an established labour organiser. What were his views on workers and strikes?

Gandhi returned from South Africa at a time of continuous labour unrest.[210] The textile industry had done well for itself during the First World War, but the prosperity was not reflected in workers' wages. In February 1918, millworkers in Ahmedabad went on strike. To mediate the dispute, Ambalal Sarabhai, president of the Ahmedabad Mill Owners' Association, turned to Gandhi, who had set up his ashram in Sabarmati, just outside Ahmedabad. It was the beginning of Gandhi's lifelong career as a labour union organiser in India. By 1920, he had managed to set up a labour union called the Majoor Mahajan Sangh—which translates as the Workers and Mill-Owners Association. The English name was the Textile Labour Union. Anusuyaben, Ambalal Sarabhai's sister, a labour organiser, was elected president for life, and Gandhi became a pivotal member of the advisory committee, also for life. The union did work at improving the hygiene and living conditions of workers, but no worker was ever elected to the union leadership. No worker was permitted to be present at closed-door arbitrations between the management and the union. The union was divided up into a federation of smaller, occupation-based unions whose members worked in the different stages of the production process. In other words, the structure of the union institutionalised caste divisions. According to a worker interviewed by the scholar Jan Breman, Untouchables were not allowed into the common canteen, they had separate drinking water tanks and segregated housing.[211]

In the union, Gandhi was the prime organiser, negotiator and decision-maker. In 1921, when workers did not turn up for work for three days, Gandhi was infuriated:

> Hindu and Muslim workers have dishonoured and humiliated themselves by abstaining from mills. Labour cannot discount me. I believe no one in India can do so. I am trying to free India from bondage and I refuse to be enslaved by workers.[212]

Here is a 1925 entry from a report of the Textile Labour Union. We don't know who wrote it, but its content and its literary cadence are unmistakably similar to what Gandhi had said about indentured labour in South Africa more than thirty years before:

> They are not as a rule armed with sufficient intelligence and moral development to resist the degrading influences which surround them on all sides in a city like this. So many of them sink in one way or another. A large number of them lose their moral balance and become slaves to liquor habits, many go down as physical wrecks and waste away from tuberculosis.[213]

Since Gandhi's main sponsor was a mill-owner and his main constituency was supposed to be the labouring class, Gandhi developed a convoluted thesis on capitalists and the working class:

> The mill-owner may be wholly in the wrong. In the struggle between capital and labour, it may be generally said that more often than not capitalists are in the wrong box. But when labour comes fully to realise its strength, I know it can become more tyrannical than capital. The mill-owners will have to work on the terms dictated by labour, if the latter could command the intelligence of the former. It is clear, however, that labour will never attain to that intelligence... It would be suicidal if the labourers rely upon their numbers or brute-force, i.e., violence. By doing so they would do harm to industries in the country. If on the other hand they take their stand on pure justice and suffer in their person to secure it, not only will they always succeed but they will reform their masters, develop industries, and both masters and men will be as members of one and the same family.[214]

Gandhi took a dim view of strikes. But his views on sweepers' strikes, which he published in 1946, were even more stringent than those on other workers' strikes:

> There are certain matters on which strikes would be wrong. Sweepers' grievances come in this category. My opinion against sweepers' strikes dates back to about 1897 when I was in Durban. A general strike was mooted there, and the question arose as to whether scavengers should join it. My vote was registered against the proposal. Just as a man cannot live without air, so too he cannot exist for long if his home and surroundings are not clean. One or the other epidemic is bound to break out, especially when modern drainage is put out of action... A Bhangi [scavenger] may not give up his work even for a day. And there are many other ways open to him for securing justice.[215]

It's not clear what the "other" ways were for securing justice: Untouchables on satyagraha were committing duragraha. Sweepers on strike were sinning. Everything other than 'sweet persuasion' was unacceptable.

While workers could not strike for fair wages, it was perfectly correct for Gandhi to be generously sponsored by big industrialists. (It was with this same sense of exceptionalism that in his reply to *Annihilation of Caste* he wrote, as point number one, "He [Ambedkar] has priced it at 8 annas, I would have advised 2 or at least 4 annas".)

▼

The differences between Ambedkar and the new Communist Party of India were not superficial. They went back to first principles. Communists were people of The Book, and The Book was written by a German Jew who had heard of, but had not actually encountered, Brahminism. This left Indian communists without theoretical tools to deal with caste. Since they were people of The Book, and since the caste system had denied Shudra and Untouchable castes the opportunity of learning, by default the leaders of the Communist Party of India and its subsequent offshoots belonged to (and by and large continue to belong to) the privileged castes, mostly Brahmin. Despite intentions that may have been genuinely revolutionary, it was not just theoretical tools they lacked, but also a ground-level understanding and empathy with 'the masses' who belonged to the subordinated castes. While Ambedkar believed that class was an important—and even primary—prism through which to view and understand society, he did not believe it was the only one. Ambedkar believed that the two enemies of the Indian working class were capitalism (in the liberal sense of the word) *and* Brahminism. Reflecting perhaps on his experience in the 1928 textile workers' strike, in *Annihilation of Caste* he asks:

> That seizure of power must be by a proletariat. The first question I ask is: Will the proletariat of India combine to bring about this revolution?... Can it be said that the proletariat of India, poor as it is, recognises no distinctions except that of the rich and poor? Can it be said that the poor in India recognise no such distinctions of caste or creed, high or low?[216]

To Indian communists, who treated caste as a sort of folk dialect derived from the classical language of class analysis, rather than as a unique, fully developed language of its own, Ambedkar said, "[T]he caste system is not merely a division of labour. *It is also a division of labourers*".[217]

Unable to reconcile his differences with the communists, and still looking for a political home for his ideas, Ambedkar decided to try and build one himself. In 1938, he founded his own political party, the Independent Labour Party (ILP). As its name suggests, the programme of the ILP was broad-based, overtly socialist and was not limited to issues of caste.

Its manifesto announced "the principle of State management and State ownership of industry whenever it may become necessary in the interests of the people". It promised a separation between the judiciary and the executive. It said it would set up land mortgage banks, agriculturist producers' cooperatives and marketing societies.[218] Though it was a young party, the ILP did extremely well in the 1937 elections, winning sixteen of the eighteen seats it contested in the Bombay Presidency and the Central Provinces and Berar. In 1939, the British government, without consulting any Indians, declared that India was at war with Germany. In protest, the Congress party resigned from all provincial ministries and the provincial assemblies were dissolved. The brief but vigorous political life of the ILP came to an abrupt end.

Angered by Ambedkar's display of independence, the communists denounced him as an 'opportunist' and an 'imperial stooge'. In his book *History of the Indian Freedom Struggle*, E.M.S. Namboodiripad, the (Brahmin) former Chief Minister of Kerala and head of the first ever democratically elected communist government in the world, wrote about the conflict between Ambedkar and the left: "However, this was a great blow to the freedom movement. For this led to the diversion of the peoples' attention from the objective of full independence to the *mundane cause* of the uplift of Harijans [Untouchables]".[219]

The rift has not mended and has harmed both sides mortally. For a brief period in the 1970s, the Dalit Panthers in Maharashtra tried to bridge the gap. They were the progeny of Ambedkar the radical (as opposed to Ambedkar the writer of the Constitution). They gave the Marathi word 'Dalit'—oppressed, broken—an all-India currency, and used it to refer not just to Untouchable communities, but to "the working people, the landless and poor peasants, women and all those who are being exploited politically and economically and in the name of religion".[220] This was a phenomenal and politically confident act of solidarity on their part. They saw Dalits as a Nation of the Oppressed. They identified their friends as "revolutionary parties set to break down the caste system and class rule" and "Left parties that are left in the true sense"; and their enemies as "Landlords, Capitalists, moneylenders and their lackeys". Their manifesto, essential reading for students of radical politics, fused the thinking of Ambedkar, Phule and Marx. The founders of the Dalit Panthers—Namdeo Dhasal, Arun Kamble and Raja Dhale—were writers and poets, and their work created a renaissance in Marathi literature.

It could have been the beginning of the revolution that India needed and is still waiting for, but the Dalit Panthers swiftly lost their bearings and disintegrated.

The caste–class question is not an easy one for political parties to address. The Communist Party's theoretical obtuseness to caste has lost it what ought to have been its natural constituency. The Communist Party of India and its offshoot, the Communist Party of India (Marxist), have more or less become bourgeois parties enmeshed in parliamentary politics. Those that split away from them in the late 1960s and independent Marxist-Leninist parties in other states (collectively known as the 'Naxalites', named after the first uprising in the village of Naxalbari in West Bengal) have tried to address the issue of caste and to make common cause with Dalits, but with little success. The few efforts they made to seize land from big zamindars and redistribute it to labourers failed because they did not have the mass support or the military firepower to see it through. Their sidelong nod to caste as opposed to a direct engagement with it has meant that even radical communist parties have lost the support of what could have been a truly militant and revolutionary constituency.

Dalits have been fragmented and pitted against each other. Many have had to move either into mainstream parliamentary politics or—with the public sector being hollowed out, and job opportunities in the private sector being denied to them—into the world of NGOs, with grants from the European Union, the Ford Foundation and other funding agencies with a long, self-serving history of defusing radical movements and harnessing them to 'market forces'.[221] There is no doubt that this funding has given a few Dalits an opportunity to be educated in what are thought to be the world's best universities. (This, after all, is what made Ambedkar the man he was.) However, even here, the Dalits' share in the massive NGO money-pie is minuscule. And within these institutions (some of which are generously funded by big corporations to work on issues of caste discrimination,[222] like Gandhi was), Dalits can be treated in unfair and ugly ways.

▼

In his search for primitive communism, S.A. Dange would have been better advised to look towards indigenous Adivasi communities rather than towards the ancient Vedic Brahmins and their yagnyas. Gandhi too could have done the same. If anybody was even remotely living out his ideal of frugal village life, of stepping lightly on the earth, it was not the Vedic Hindus, it was the Adivasis. For them, however, Gandhi showed the same level of disdain that he did for Black Africans. Speaking in 1896 at a public meeting in Bombay, he said: "The Santhals of Assam will be as useless in South Africa as the natives of that country".[223]

On the Adivasi question, Ambedkar too stumbles. So quick to react to slights against his own people, Ambedkar, in a passage in *Annihilation of Caste*, echoes the thinking of colonial missionaries and liberal ideologues, and adds his own touch of Brahminism:

Thirteen million people living in the midst of civilisation are still in a savage state, and are leading the life of hereditary criminals... The Hindus will probably seek to account for this savage state of the aborigines by attributing to them congenital stupidity. They will probably not admit that the aborigines have remained savages because they made no effort to civilise them, to give them medical aid, to reform them, to make them good citizens... Civilising the aborigines means adopting them as your own, living in their midst, and cultivating fellow-feeling—in short, loving them...

The Hindu has not realised that these aborigines are a source of potential danger. If these savages remain savages, they may not do any harm to the Hindus. But if they are reclaimed by non-Hindus and converted to their faiths, they will swell the ranks of the enemies of the Hindus.[224]

Today, Adivasis are the barricade against the pitiless march of modern capitalism. Their very existence poses the most radical questions about modernity and 'progress'—the ideas that Ambedkar embraced as one of the ways out of the caste system. Unfortunately, by viewing the Adivasi community through the lens of Western liberalism, Ambedkar's writing, which is otherwise so relevant in today's context, suddenly becomes dated.

Ambedkar's opinions about Adivasis betrayed a lack of information and understanding. First of all, Hindu evangelists like the Hindu Mahasabha had been working to 'assimilate' the Adivasis since the 1920s (just like they were Balmiki-ising castes that were forced into cleaning and scavenging work). Tribes like the Ho, the Oraon, the Kols, the Santhals, the Mundas and the Gonds did not wish to be 'civilised' or 'assimilated'. They had rebelled time and again against the British as well as against zamindars and Bania moneylenders, and had fought fiercely to protect their land, culture and heritage. Thousands had been killed in these uprisings, but unlike the rest of India, they were never conquered. They still have not been. Today, they are the armed, militant end of a spectrum of struggles. They are waging nothing short of a civil war against the Indian state which has signed over Adivasi homelands to infrastructure and mining corporations. They are the backbone of the decades-long struggle against big dams in the Narmada Valley. They make up the ranks of the People's Liberation Guerrilla Army of the Communist Party of India (Maoist) that is fighting tens of thousands of paramilitary forces that have been deployed by the government in the forests of Central India.

In a 1945 address in Bombay ("The Communal Deadlock and a Way to Solve It"), discussing the issue of proportionate representation, Ambedkar brought up the issue of Adivasi rights once again. He said:

> My proposals do not cover the Aboriginal Tribes although they are larger in number than the Sikhs, Anglo-Indians, Indian Christians and Parsis... The Aboriginal Tribes have not as yet developed any political sense to make the best use of their political opportunities and they may easily become mere instruments in the hands either of a majority or a minority and thereby disturb the balance without doing any good to themselves.[225]

This unfortunate way of describing a community was sometimes aimed at non-Adivasis too, in an equally troubling manner. At one point in *Annihilation of Caste* Ambedkar resorts to using the language of eugenics, a subject that was popular with European fascists: "Physically speaking the Hindus are a C3 people. They are a race of pygmies and dwarfs, stunted in stature and wanting in stamina".[226]

His views on Adivasis had serious consequences. In 1950, the Indian Constitution made the state the custodian of Adivasi homelands, thereby ratifying British colonial policy. The Adivasi population became squatters on their own land. By denying them their traditional rights to forest produce, it criminalised a whole way of life. It gave them the right to vote, but snatched away their livelihood and dignity.[227]

How different are Ambedkar's words on Adivasis from Gandhi's words on Untouchables when he said:

> Muslims and Sikhs are all well organised. The 'Untouchables' are not. There is very little political consciousness among them, and they are so horribly treated that I want to save them against themselves. If they had separate electorates, their lives would be miserable in villages which are the strongholds of Hindu orthodoxy. It is the superior class of Hindus who have to do penance for having neglected the 'Untouchables' for ages. That penance can be done by active social reform and by making the lot of the 'Untouchables' more bearable by acts of service, but not by asking for separate electorates for them.[228]

Gandhi said this at the Second Round Table Conference in London in 1931. It was the first public face-to-face encounter between Ambedkar and Gandhi.

THE CONFRONTATION

The Congress had boycotted the First Round Table Conference in 1930, but nominated Gandhi as its representative in the second. The aim of the conference was to frame a new constitution for self-rule. The princely states and representatives of various minority communities—Muslims, Sikhs, Christians, Parsis and Untouchables—were present. Adivasis went unrepresented. For Untouchables, it was a historic occasion. It was the first time that they had been invited as a separately represented constituency. One of the several committees that made up the conference was the Minority Committee, charged with the task of finding a workable solution to the growing communal question. It was potentially the most inflammable and, perhaps for that reason, was chaired by the British Prime Minister, Ramsay MacDonald.

It was to this committee that Ambedkar submitted his memorandum, which he described as *A Scheme of Political Safeguards for the Protection of the Depressed Classes in the Future Constitution of a Self-Governing India*. It was, for its time, within the framework of liberal debates on rights and citizenship, a revolutionary document. In it, Ambedkar tried to do in law what he dreamt of achieving socially and politically. This document was an early draft of some of the ideas that Ambedkar eventually managed to put into the Constitution of post-1947 India.

Under "Condition No. 1: Equal Citizenship", it says:

> The Depressed Classes cannot consent to subject themselves to majority rule in their present state of hereditary bondsmen. Before majority rule is established, their emancipation from the system of untouchability must be an accomplished fact. It must not be left to the will of the majority. The Depressed Classes must be made free citizens entitled to all the rights of citizenship in common with other citizens of the State.[229]

The memorandum went on to delineate what would constitute Fundamental Rights and how they were to be protected. It gave Untouchables the right to access all public places. It dwelt at length on social boycotts and suggested they be declared a criminal offence. It prescribed a series of measures by which Untouchables would be protected from social boycotts and caste Hindus punished for instigating and promoting them. Condition No. 5 asked that a Public Service Commission be set up to ensure Untouchables "Adequate Representation in the Services". This is what has eventually evolved into the system of reservation in educational institutions and government jobs, against which privileged castes in recent times have militantly agitated.[230]

The most unique aspect of Ambedkar's memorandum was

his proposal for a system of positive discrimination within the electoral system. Ambedkar did not believe that universal adult franchise alone could secure equal rights for Untouchables. Since the Untouchable population was scattered across the country in little settlements on the outskirts of Hindu villages, Ambedkar realised that within the geographical demarcation of a political constituency, they would always be a minority and would never be in a position to elect a candidate of their own choice. He suggested that Untouchables, who had been despised and devalued for so many centuries, be given a separate electorate so that they could, without interference from the Hindu orthodoxy, develop into a political constituency with a leadership of its own. In addition to this, and in order that they retain their connection with mainstream politics, he suggested that they be given the right to vote for general candidates too. Both the separate electorate and the double vote were to last for a period of only ten years. Though the details were not agreed upon, when the conference concluded, all the delegates unanimously agreed that the Untouchables should, like the other minorities, have a separate electorate.[231]

While the First Round Table Conference was in session in London, India was in turmoil. In January 1930, the Congress had declared its demand for Poorna Swaraj—complete independence. Gandhi showcased his genius as a political organiser and launched his most imaginative political action yet—the Salt Satyagraha. He called on Indians to march to the sea and break the British salt tax laws. Hundreds of thousands of Indians rallied to his call. Jails filled to overflowing. Ninety thousand people were arrested. Between salt and water, between the Touchables' satyagraha and the Untouchables' 'duragraha' lay a sharply divided universe—of politics, of philosophy and of morality.

At its Karachi Session in March 1931, the Congress passed

a Resolution of Fundamental Rights for a free India.[232] It was a valuable, enlightened document, and it included some of the rights Ambedkar had been campaigning for. It laid the foundation for a modern, secular and largely socialist state. The rights included the freedoms of speech, press, assembly and association, equality before law, universal adult franchise, free and compulsory primary education, a guaranteed living wage for every citizen and limited hours of work. It underlined the protection of women and peasants, and state ownership or control of key industries, mines and transport. Most important, it created a firewall between religion and the state.

Notwithstanding the admirable principles of the Resolution of Fundamental Rights that had been passed, the view from the bottom was slightly different. The 1930 elections to the provincial legislatures coincided with the Salt Satyagraha. The Congress had boycotted the elections. In order to embarrass 'respectable' Hindus who did not heed the boycott and stood as independent candidates, the Congress fielded mock candidates who were Untouchables—two cobblers, a barber, a milkman and a sweeper. The idea was that no self-respecting, privileged-caste Hindu would want to be part of an institution where he or she was put on a par with Untouchables.[233] Putting up Untouchables as mock candidates was a Congress party tactic that had begun with the 1920 elections and went on right up to 1943. Ambedkar says:

> What were the means adopted by the Congress to prevent Hindus from standing on an independent ticket? The means were to make the legislatures objects of contempt. Accordingly, the Congress, in various provinces, started processions carrying placards saying, 'Who will go to the Legislatures? Only barbers, cobblers, potters and sweepers.' In the processions, one man would utter the question as part of the slogan and the whole crowd would repeat as answer the second part of the slogan.[234]

At the Round Table Conference, Gandhi and Ambedkar

clashed, both claiming that they were the real representatives of the Untouchables. The conference went on for weeks. Gandhi eventually agreed to separate electorates for Muslims and Sikhs, but would not countenance Ambedkar's argument for a separate electorate for Untouchables. He resorted to his usual rhetoric: "I would far rather that Hinduism died than that Untouchability lived".[235]

Gandhi refused to acknowledge that Ambedkar had the right to represent Untouchables. Ambedkar would not back down either. Nor was there a call for him to. Untouchable groups from across India, including Mangoo Ram of the Ad Dharm movement, sent telegrams in support of Ambedkar. Eventually Gandhi said, "Those who speak of the political rights of Untouchables do not know their India, do not know how Indian society is today constructed, and therefore I want to say with all the emphasis that I can command that if I was the only person to resist this thing I would resist it with my life".[236] Having delivered his threat, Gandhi took the boat back to India. On the way, he dropped in on Mussolini in Rome and was extremely impressed by him and his "care of the poor, his opposition to super-urbanisation, his efforts to bring about co-ordination between capital and labour".[237]

A year later, Ramsay MacDonald announced the British government's decision on the Communal Question. It awarded the Untouchables a separate electorate for a period of twenty years. At the time, Gandhi was serving a sentence in Yerawada Central Jail in Poona. From prison, he announced that unless the provision of separate electorates for Untouchables was revoked, he would fast to death.

He waited for a month. When he did not get his way, Gandhi began his fast from prison. This fast was completely against his own maxims of satyagraha. It was barefaced blackmail, nothing less manipulative than the threat of committing public suicide.

The British government said it would revoke the provision only if the Untouchables agreed. The country spun like a top. Public statements were issued, petitions signed, prayers offered, meetings held, appeals made. It was a preposterous situation: privileged-caste Hindus, who segregated themselves from Untouchables in every possible way, who deemed them unworthy of human association, who shunned their very touch, who wanted separate food, water, schools, roads, temples and wells, now said that India would be balkanised if Untouchables had a separate electorate. And Gandhi, who believed so fervently and so vocally in the system that upheld that separation was starving himself to death to deny Untouchables a separate electorate.

The gist of it was that the caste Hindus wanted the power to close the door on Untouchables, but on no account could Untouchables be given the power to close the door on themselves. The masters knew that choice was power.

As the frenzy mounted, Ambedkar became the villain, the traitor, the man who wanted to dissever India, the man who was trying to kill Gandhi. Political heavyweights of the garam dal (militants) as well as the naram dal (moderates), including Tagore, Nehru and C. Rajagopalachari, weighed in on Gandhi's side. To placate Gandhi, privileged-caste Hindus made a show of sharing food on the streets with Untouchables, and many Hindu temples were thrown open to them, albeit temporarily. Behind those gestures of accommodation, a wall of tension built up too. Several Untouchable leaders feared that Ambedkar would be held responsible if Gandhi succumbed to his fast, and this in turn, could put the lives of ordinary Untouchables in danger. One of them was M.C. Rajah, the Untouchable leader from Madras, who, according to an eyewitness account of the events, said:

For thousands of years we had been treated as Untouchables,

downtrodden, insulted, despised. The Mahatma is staking his life for our sake, and if he dies, for the next thousands of years we shall be where we have been, if not worse. There will be such a strong feeling against us that we brought about his death, that the mind of the whole Hindu community and the whole civilised community will kick us downstairs further still. I am not going to stand by you any longer. I will join the conference and find a solution and I will part company from you.[238]

What could Ambedkar do? He tried to hold out with his usual arsenal of logic and reason, but the situation was way beyond all that. He didn't stand a chance. After four days of the fast, on 24 September 1932, Ambedkar visited Gandhi in Yerawada prison and signed the Poona Pact. The next day in Bombay he made a public speech in which he was uncharacteristically gracious about Gandhi: "I was astounded to see that the man who held such divergent views from mine at the Round Table Conference came immediately to my rescue and not to the rescue of the other side".[239]

Later, though, having recovered from the trauma, Ambedkar wrote:

There was nothing noble in the fast. It was a foul and filthy act… [I]t was the worst form of coercion against a helpless people to give up the constitutional safeguards of which they had become possessed under the Prime Minister's Award and agree to live on the mercy of the Hindus. It was a vile and wicked act. How can the Untouchables regard such a man as honest and sincere?[240]

According to the Pact, instead of separate electorates, the Untouchables would have reserved seats in general constituencies. The number of seats they were allotted in the provincial legislatures increased (from seventy-eight to 148), but the candidates, because they would now have to be acceptable to their privileged caste–dominated constituencies, lost their teeth.[241] Uncle Tom won the day. Gandhi saw to it that leadership remained in the hands of the privileged castes.

In *The New Jim Crow*, Michelle Alexander[242] describes how, in the United States, criminalisation and mass incarceration has led to the disenfranchisement of an extraordinary percentage of the African American population. In India, in a far slyer way, an apparently generous form of enfranchisement has ensured the virtual disenfranchisement of the Dalit population.

Nevertheless, what to Ambedkar was a foul and filthy act appeared to others as nothing less than a divine miracle. Louis Fischer, author of perhaps the most widely read biography of Gandhi ever written, said:

> The fast could not kill the curse of untouchability which was more than three thousand years old ... but after the fast, untouchability forfeited its public approval; the belief in it was destroyed... Gandhi's 'Epic Fast' snapped a long chain that stretched back into antiquity and had enslaved tens of millions. Some links of the chain remained. Many wounds from the chain remained. But nobody would forge new links, nobody would link the links together again... It [the Poona Pact] marked a religious reformation, a psychological revolution. Hinduism was purging itself of a millennial sickness. The mass purified itself in practice... If Gandhi had done nothing else in his life but shatter the structure of untouchability he would have been a great social reformer... Gandhi's agony gave vicarious pain to his adorers who knew they must not kill God's messenger on earth. It was evil to prolong his suffering. It was blessed to save him by being good to those whom he had called 'The Children of God'.[243]

On the great occasion of the Poona Pact, contradicting the stand he took at the Round Table Conference, Gandhi was quite willing to accept Ambedkar's signature on the pact as the representative of the Untouchables. Gandhi himself did not sign the pact, but the list of the other signatories is interesting: G.D. Birla, Gandhi's industrialist-patron; Pandit Madan Mohan

Malaviya, a conservative Brahmin leader and founder of the right-wing Hindu Mahasabha (of which Gandhi's future assassin, Nathuram Godse, was a member); V.D. Savarkar, accused of conspiracy in Gandhi's assassination, who also served as president of the Mahasabha; Palwankar Baloo, an Untouchable cricketer of the Chambhar caste, who was celebrated earlier as a sporting idol by Ambedkar, and whom the Congress and the Hindu Mahasabha propped up as an opponent of Ambedkar;[244] and, of course, M.C. Rajah (who would, much later, regret his collusion with Gandhi, the Hindu Mahasabha and the Congress).[245]

Among the (many) reasons that criticism of Gandhi is not just frowned upon, but often censored in India, 'secularists' tell us, is that Hindu nationalists (from whose midst Gandhi's assassins arose, and whose star is on the ascendant in India these days) will seize upon such criticism and turn it to their advantage. The fact is there was never much daylight between Gandhi's views on caste and those of the Hindu right. From a Dalit point of view, Gandhi's assassination could appear to be more a fratricidal killing than an assassination by an ideological opponent. Even today, Narendra Modi, Hindu nationalism's most aggressive proponent, and a possible future prime minister, is able to invoke Gandhi in his public speeches without the slightest discomfort.* (Modi invoked Gandhi to justify the introduction of two anti-minority legislations in Gujarat—the anti-conversion law of 2003, called the Gujarat Freedom of Religion Act, and the amendment to the old cow-slaughter law in 2011.[246]) Many of Modi's pronouncements are delivered from the Mahatma Mandir in Gandhinagar, a spanking new convention hall whose foundation contains sand brought in special urns from each of Gujarat's 18,000 villages, many of which continue to practise egregious forms of untouchability.[247]

---

* In 2014 Modi was elected Prime Minister of India.

After the Poona Pact, Gandhi directed all his energy and passion towards the eradication of untouchability. For a start, he rebaptised Untouchables and gave them a patronising name: Harijans. 'Hari' is the name for a male deity in Hinduism, 'jan' is people. So Harijans are People of God, though in order to infantilise them even further, in translation they are referred to as 'Children of God'. In this way, Gandhi anchored Untouchables firmly to the Hindu faith.[248] He founded a new newspaper called *Harijan*. He started the Harijan Sevak Sangh (Harijan Service Society), which he insisted would be manned only by privileged-caste Hindus who had to do penance for their past sins against Untouchables. Ambedkar saw all this as the Congress's plan to "kill Untouchables by kindness".[249]

Gandhi toured the country, preaching against untouchability. He was heckled and attacked by Hindus even more conservative than himself, but he did not swerve from his purpose. Everything that happened was harnessed to the cause of eradicating caste. In January 1934, there was a major earthquake in Bihar. Almost twenty thousand people lost their lives. Writing in the *Harijan* on 24 February, Gandhi shocked even his colleagues in the Congress when he said it was God's punishment to the people for the sin of practising untouchability. None of this stopped the Congress party from continuing with a tradition it had invented: it once again fielded mock Untouchable candidates in the 1934 elections to the Central Legislature.[250]

Gandhi could not, it appears, conceive of a role for Untouchables other than as victims in need of ministration. That they had also been psychologically hardwired into the caste system, that they too might need to be roused out of thousands of years of being conditioned to think of themselves as subhuman, was an antithetical, intimidating idea to Gandhi. The Poona Pact was meant to defuse or at least delay the political awakening of Untouchables.

What Gandhi's campaign against untouchability did, and did effectively, was to rub balm on injuries that were centuries old. To a vast mass of Untouchables, accustomed only to being terrorised, shunned and brutalised, this missionary activity would have induced feelings of gratitude and even worship. Gandhi knew that. He was a politician. Ambedkar was not. Or, at any rate, not a very good one. Gandhi knew how to make charity an event, a piece of theatre, a spectacular display of fireworks. So, while the Doctor was searching for a more lasting cure, the Saint journeyed across India distributing a placebo.

The chief concern of the Harijan Sevak Sangh was to persuade privileged castes to open up temples to Untouchables—ironic, because Gandhi was no temple-goer himself. Nor was his sponsor G.D. Birla, who, in an interview with Margaret Bourke-White, said, "Frankly speaking, we build temples but we don't believe in temples. We build temples to spread a kind of religious mentality".[251] The opening of temples had already begun during the days of Gandhi's epic fast. Under pressure from the Harijan Sevak Sangh, hundreds of temples were thrown open to Untouchables. (Some, like the Guruvayur temple in Kerala, refused point-blank. Gandhi contemplated a fast but soon changed his mind.[252]) Others announced that they were open to Untouchables but found ways of humiliating them and making it impossible for them to enter with any sort of dignity.

A Temple Entry Bill was tabled in the Central Legislature in 1933. Gandhi and the Congress supported it enthusiastically. But when it became apparent that the privileged castes were seriously opposed to it, they backed out.[253]

Ambedkar was sceptical about the temple entry programme. He saw that it had a tremendous psychological impact on Untouchables, but he recognised temple entry as the beginning of 'assimilation'—of Hinduising and Brahminising Untouchables, drawing them further into being partners in their own humiliation.

If the "infection of imitation" of Brahminism had been implanted in Untouchables even when they had been denied entry into temples for centuries, what would temple entry do for them? On 14 February 1933, Ambedkar issued a statement on temple entry:

> What the Depressed Classes want is a religion that will give them equality of social status ... nothing can be more odious and vile than that admitted social evils should be sought to be justified on the ground of religion. The Depressed Classes may not be able to overthrow inequities to which they are subjected. But they have made up their mind not to tolerate a religion that will lend its support to the continuance of these inequities.[254]

Ambedkar was only echoing what a fourteen-year-old Untouchable Mang girl, Muktabai Salve, had said long ago. She was a student in the school for Untouchable children that Jotiba and Savitri Phule ran in Poona. In 1855, she said, "Let that religion, where only one person is privileged and the rest are deprived, perish from the earth and let it never enter our minds to be proud of such a religion".[255]

Ambedkar had learned from experience that Christianity, Sikhism, Islam and Zoroastrianism were not impervious to caste discrimination. In 1934, he had a reprise of his old experiences. He was visiting the Daulatabad fort, in the princely state of Hyderabad, with a group of friends and co-workers. It was the month of Ramzan. Dusty and tired from their journey, Ambedkar and his friends stopped to drink water and wash their faces from a public tank. They were surrounded by a mob of angry Muslims calling them 'Dheds' (a derogatory term for Untouchables). They were abused, nearly assaulted and prevented from touching the water. "This will show," Ambedkar writes in his *Autobiographical Notes*, "that a person who is Untouchable to a Hindu, is also Untouchable to a Mohammedan".[256]

A new spiritual home was nowhere in sight.

Still, at the 1935 Yeola conference, Ambedkar renounced Hinduism. In 1936, he published the incendiary (and overpriced, as Gandhi patronisingly commented) text of *Annihilation of Caste* that set out the reasons for why he had done so.

That same year, Gandhiji too made a memorable contribution to literature. He was by now sixty-eight years old. He wrote a classic essay called "The Ideal Bhangi":

> The Brahmin's duty is to look after the sanitation of the soul, the Bhangi's that of the body of society ... and yet our woebegone Indian society has branded the Bhangi as a social pariah, set him down at the bottom of the scale, held him fit only to receive kicks and abuse, a creature who must subsist on the leavings of the caste people and dwell on the dung heap.
>
> If only we had given due recognition to the status of the Bhangi as equal to that of the Brahmin, our villages, no less their inhabitants would have looked a picture of cleanliness and order. I therefore make bold to state without any manner of hesitation or doubt that not till the invidious distinction between Brahmin and Bhangi is removed will our society enjoy health, prosperity and peace and be happy.

He then outlined the educational requirements, practical skills and etiquette an ideal Bhangi should possess:

> What qualities therefore should such an honoured servant of society exemplify in his person? In my opinion an ideal Bhangi should have a thorough knowledge of the principles of sanitation. He should know how a right kind of latrine is constructed and the correct way of cleaning it. He should know how to overcome and destroy the odour of excreta and the various disinfectants to render them innocuous. He should likewise know the process of converting urine and night soil into manure. But that is not all. My ideal Bhangi would know the quality of night soil and urine. He would keep a close watch on these and give timely warning to the individual concerned...

The *Manusmriti* says a Shudra should not amass wealth even if he has the ability, for a Shudra who amasses wealth annoys the Brahmin.[257] Gandhi, a Bania, for whom the *Manusmriti* prescribes usury as a divine calling, says: "Such an ideal Bhangi, while deriving his livelihood from his occupation, would approach it only as a sacred duty. In other words, he would not dream of amassing wealth out of it."[258]

Seventy years later, in his book *Karmayogi* (which he withdrew after the Balmiki community protested), Narendra Modi proved he was a diligent disciple of the Mahatma:

> I do not believe they have been doing this job just to sustain their livelihood. Had this been so, they would not have continued with this kind of job generation after generation... At some point of time somebody must have got the enlightenment that it is their (Balmikis') duty to work for the happiness of the entire society and the Gods; that they have to do this job bestowed upon them by Gods; and this job should continue as internal spiritual activity for centuries.[259]

The naram dal and the garam dal may be separate political parties today, but ideologically they are not as far apart from each other as we think they are.

Like all the other Hindu reformers, Gandhi too was alarmed by Ambedkar's talk of renouncing Hinduism. He adamantly opposed the religious conversion of Untouchables. In November 1936, in a now-famous conversation with John Mott—an American evangelist and chairman of the International Missionary Council—Gandhi said:

> It hurt me to find Christian bodies vying with the Muslims and Sikhs in trying to add to the numbers of their fold. It seemed to me an ugly performance and a travesty of religion. They even proceeded to enter into secret conclaves with Dr Ambedkar. I should have understood and appreciated your prayers for the Harijans, but instead you made an appeal to those who had not

even the mind and intelligence to understand what you talked; they have certainly not the intelligence to distinguish between Jesus and Mohammed and Nanak and so on… If Christians want to associate themselves with this reform movement they should do so without any idea of conversion.

J.M.: Apart from this unseemly competition, should they not preach the Gospel with reference to its acceptance?

G: Would you, Dr Mott, preach the Gospel to a cow? Well, some of the untouchables are worse than cows in understanding. I mean they can no more distinguish between the relative merits of Islam and Hinduism and Christianity than a cow. You can only preach through your life. The rose does not say: 'Come and smell me'.[260]

It's true that Gandhi often contradicted himself. It's also true that he was capable of being remarkably consistent. For more than half a century—throughout his adult life—his pronouncements on the inherent qualities of Black Africans, Untouchables and the labouring classes remained consistently insulting. His refusal to allow working-class people and Untouchables to create their own political organisations and elect their own representatives (which Ambedkar considered to be fundamental to the notion of citizenship) remained consistent too.[261]

Gandhi's political instincts served the Congress party extremely well. His campaign of temple entry drew the Untouchable population in great numbers to the Congress.

Though Ambedkar had a formidable intellect, he didn't have the sense of timing, the duplicity, the craftiness and the ability to be unscrupulous—qualities that a good politician needs. His constituency was made up of the poorest, most oppressed sections of the population. He had no financial backing. In 1942, Ambedkar reconfigured the Independent Labour Party into the much more self-limiting Scheduled Castes Federation. The timing was wrong. By then, the national movement was reigniting. Gandhi had announced the Quit India Movement.

The Muslim League's demand for Pakistan was gaining traction, and for a while caste identity became less important that the Hindu–Muslim issue.

By the mid-1940s, as the prospect of partition loomed, the subordinated castes in several states had been 'assimilated' into Hinduism. They began to participate in militant Hindu rallies; in Noakhali in Bengal, for instance, they functioned as an outlying vigilante army in the run-up to the bloodbath of partition.[262]

In 1947 Pakistan became the world's first Islamic republic. More than six decades later, as the War on Terror continues in its many avatars, political Islam is turning inwards, narrowing and hardening its precincts. Meanwhile, political Hinduism is expanding and broadening. Today, even the Bhakti movement has been 'assimilated' as a form of popular, folk Hinduism.[263] The naram dal, often dressed up as 'secular nationalism', has recruited Jotiba Phule, Pandita Ramabai and even Ambedkar, all of whom denounced Hinduism, back into the 'Hindu fold' as people Hindus can be 'proud' of.[264] Ambedkar is being assimilated in another way too—as Gandhi's junior partner in their joint fight against untouchability.

The anxiety around demography has by no means abated. Hindu supremacist organisations like the Rashtriya Swayamsevak Sangh and the Shiv Sena are working hard (and successfully) at luring Dalits and Adivasis into the 'Hindu fold'. In the forests of Central India, where a corporate war for minerals is raging, the Vishwa Hindu Parishad (VHP) and the Bajrang Dal (both organisations that are loosely linked to the RSS) run mass conversion programmes called 'ghar wapsi'— the return home—in which Adivasi people are 'reconverted' to Hinduism. Privileged-caste Hindus, who pride themselves on being descendants of Aryan invaders, are busy persuading people who belong to indigenous, autochthonous tribes to return 'home'.

It makes you feel that irony is no longer a literary option in this part of the world.

Dalits who have been harnessed to the 'Hindu fold' serve another purpose: even if they have not been part of the outlying army, they can be used as scapegoats for the crimes the privileged castes commit.

In 2002, in the Godhra railway station in Gujarat, a train compartment was mysteriously burned down, and fifty-eight Hindu pilgrims were charred to death. With not much evidence to prove their guilt, some Muslims were arrested as the perpetrators. The Muslim community as a whole was collectively blamed for the crime. Over the next few days, the VHP and the Bajrang Dal led a pogrom in which more than two thousand Muslims were murdered, women were mob-raped and burnt alive in broad daylight and a hundred and fifty thousand people were driven from their homes.[265] After the pogrom, 287 people were arrested under the Prevention of Terrorism Act (POTA). Of them, 286 were Muslim and one was a Sikh.[266] Most of them are still in prison.

If Muslims were the 'terrorists', who were the 'rioters'? In his essay "Blood Under Saffron: The Myth of Dalit–Muslim Confrontation", Raju Solanki, a Gujarati Dalit writer who studied the pattern of arrests, says that of the 1,577 'Hindus' who were arrested (not under POTA of course), 747 were Dalits and 797 belonged to 'Other Backward Classes'. Nineteen were Patels, two were Banias and two were Brahmins. The massacres of Muslims occurred in several cities and villages in Gujarat. However, Solanki points out that not a single massacre took place in *bastis* where Dalits and Muslims lived together.[267]

Narendra Modi, the Chief Minister of Gujarat who presided over the pogrom, has since won the state elections three times in a row. Despite being a Shudra, he has endeared himself to the Hindu right by being more blatantly and ruthlessly anti-Muslim than any other Indian politician. When he was asked in a recent interview whether he regretted what happened in 2002, he said, "[I]f we are driving a car, we are a driver, and someone else is driving a car and we're sitting behind, even then if a puppy comes under the wheel, will it be painful or not? Of course it is. If I'm a Chief Minister or not, I'm a human being. If something bad happens anywhere, it is natural to be sad."[268]

As blatantly casteist and communal as the Hindu right is, in their search for a foothold in mainstream politics, even radical Dalits have made common cause with it. In the mid-1990s, the remarkable Dalit poet Namdeo Dhasal, one of the founders of the Dalit Panthers, joined the Shiv Sena. In 2006, Dhasal shared the dais with RSS chief K.S. Sudarshan at a book launch and praised the RSS's efforts at equality.[269]

It is easy to dismiss what Dhasal did as an unforgivable compromise with fascists. However, in parliamentary politics, after the Poona Pact—rather *because* of the Poona Pact—Dalits as a political constituency have had to make alliances with those whose interests are hostile to their own. For Dalits, as we have seen, the distance between the Hindu 'right' and the Hindu 'left' is not as great as it might appear to be to others.

Despite the debacle of the Poona Pact, Ambedkar didn't entirely give up the idea of separate electorates. Unfortunately, his second party, the Scheduled Castes Federation, was defeated in the 1946 elections to the Provincial Legislature. The defeat meant that Ambedkar lost his place on the Executive Council in the Interim Ministry that was formed in August 1946. It was a serious blow, because Ambedkar desperately wanted to use his position on the Executive Council to become part of the committee that would draft the Indian Constitution. Worried that this was not going to be possible, and in order to put external pressure on the Drafting Committee, Ambedkar, in March 1947, published a document called *States and Minorities*—

his proposed constitution for a 'United States of India' (an idea whose time has perhaps come). Fortunately for him, the Muslim League chose Jogendranath Mandal, a colleague of Ambedkar's and a Scheduled Castes Federation leader from Bengal, as one of its candidates on the Executive Council. Mandal made sure that Ambedkar was elected to the Constituent Assembly from the Bengal province. But disaster struck again. After partition, East Bengal went to Pakistan and Ambedkar lost his position once more. In a gesture of goodwill, and perhaps because there was no one as equal to the task as he was, the Congress appointed Ambedkar to the Constituent Assembly. In August 1947, Ambedkar was appointed India's first Law Minister and Chairman of the Drafting Committee for the Constitution. Across the new border, Jogendranath Mandal became Pakistan's first Law Minister.[270] It was extraordinary that, through all the chaos and prejudice, the first law ministers of both India and Pakistan were Dalits. Mandal was eventually disillusioned with Pakistan and returned to India. Ambedkar was disillusioned too, but he really had nowhere to go.

The Indian Constitution was drafted by a committee, and reflected the views of its privileged-caste members more than Ambedkar's. Still, several of the safeguards for Untouchables that he had outlined in *States and Minorities* did find their way in. Some of Ambedkar's more radical suggestions, such as nationalising agriculture and key industries, were summarily dropped. The drafting process left Ambedkar more than a little unhappy. In March 1955, he said in the Rajya Sabha (India's Upper House of Parliament): "The Constitution was a wonderful temple we built for the gods, but before they could be installed, the devils have taken possession."[271] In 1954, Ambedkar contested his last election as a Scheduled Castes Federation candidate and lost.

▼

Ambedkar was disillusioned with Hinduism, with its high priests, its saints and its politicians. Yet the response to temple entry probably taught him how much people long to belong to a spiritual community, and how inadequate a charter of civil rights or a constitution is to address those needs.

After twenty years of contemplation, during which he studied Islam as well as Christianity, Ambedkar turned to Buddhism. This, too, he entered in his own, distinct, angular way. He was wary of classical Buddhism, of the ways in which Buddhist philosophy could, had and continues to be used to justify war and unimaginable cruelty. (The most recent example is the Sri Lankan government's version of state Buddhism, which culminated in the genocidal killing of at least 40,000 ethnic Tamils and the internal displacement of 300,000 people in 2009.[272]) Ambedkar's Buddhism, called 'Navayana Buddhism'[273] or the Fourth Way, distinguished between religion and dhamma. "The purpose of Religion is to explain the origin of the world," Ambedkar said, sounding very much like Karl Marx, "the purpose of Dhamma is to reconstruct the world".[274] On 14 October 1956, in Nagpur, only months before his death, Ambedkar, Sharda Kabir, his (Brahmin) second wife, and half a million supporters took the vow of the Three Jewels and Five Precepts and converted to Buddhism. It was his most radical act. It marked his departure from Western liberalism and its purely materialistic vision of a society based on 'rights', a vision whose origin coincided with the rise of modern capitalism.

Ambedkar did not have enough money to print his major work on Buddhism, *The Buddha and His Dhamma*, before he died.[275]

He wore suits, yes. But he died in debt.

▼

Where does that leave the rest of us?

Though they call the age we are living through the Kali Yuga,[276] Ram Rajya could be just around the corner. The fourteenth-century Babri Masjid, supposedly built on the birthplace of Lord Ram in Ayodhya, was demolished by Hindu storm troopers on 6 December 1992, Ambedkar's death anniversary. We await with apprehension the construction of a grand Ram temple in its place. As Mahatma Gandhi desired, the rich man has been left in possession of his (as well as everybody else's) wealth. Chaturvarna reigns unchallenged: the Brahmin largely controls knowledge; the Vaishya dominates trade. The Kshatriyas have seen better days, but they are still, for the most part, rural landowners. The Shudras live in the basement of the Big House and keep intruders at bay. The Adivasis are fighting for their very survival. And the Dalits—well, we've been through all that.

Can caste be annihilated?

Not unless we show the courage to rearrange the stars in our firmament. Not unless those who call themselves revolutionary develop a radical critique of Brahminism. Not unless those who understand Brahminism sharpen their critique of capitalism.

And not unless we read Babasaheb Ambedkar. If not inside our classrooms, then outside them. Until then we will remain what he called the "sick men" and women of Hindustan, who seem to have no desire to get well.

Notes

1 For this account of Khairlanji, I have drawn on Anand Teltumbde (2010a). For one of the first comprehensive news reports on the incident, see Sabrina Buckwalter (2006).

2 For an analysis of the lower court judgement, see S. Anand (2008b).

3 On 11 July 1996, the Ranveer Sena, a privileged-caste, feudal militia, murdered twenty-one landless labourers in Bathani Tola village in the state of Bihar. In 2012, the Patna High Court acquitted all the accused. On 1 December 1997, the Ranveer Sena massacred fifty-eight Dalits in Laxmanpur Bathe village, also in Bihar. In April 2010, the trial court convicted all the twenty-six accused. It sentenced ten of them to life imprisonment and sixteen to death. In October 2013, the Patna High Court suspended the conviction of all twenty-six accused, saying the prosecution had not produced any evidence to guarantee any punishment at all.

4 These are some of the major crimes against Dalits and subordinated castes that have taken place in recent times: in 1968, in Keezhvenmani in the state of Tamil Nadu, forty-four Dalits were burnt alive; in 1977, in Belchi village of Bihar, fourteen Dalits were burnt alive; in 1978, in Marichjhapi, an island in the Sundarbans mangrove forest of West Bengal, hundreds of Dalit refugees from Bangladesh were massacred during a left-led government's eviction drive; in 1984, in Karamchedu in the state of Andhra Pradesh, six Dalits were murdered, three Dalit women raped and many more wounded; in 1991, in Chunduru, also in Andhra Pradesh, nine Dalits were slaughtered and their bodies dumped in a canal; in 1997, in Melavalavu in Tamil Nadu, an elected Dalit panchayat leader and five Dalits were murdered; in 2000, in Kambalapalli in the state of Karnataka, six Dalits were burnt alive; in 2002, in Jhajjar in the state of Haryana, five Dalits were lynched outside a police station. See also the documentation by Human Rights Watch (1999) and the Navsarjan report (2009).

5 BAWS 9, 296. All references to B.R. Ambedkar's writings, except

from *Annihilation of Caste*, are from the *Babasaheb Ambedkar: Writings and Speeches* (BAWS) series published by the Education Department, Government of Maharashtra. All references to *Annihilation of Caste* (henceforth AoC) are from the Navayana edition.

6   Rupa Viswanath (2012) writes, "Where 'Dalit' refers to all those Indians, past and present, traditionally regarded as outcastes and untouchable, 'SC' is a modern governmental category that explicitly excludes Christian and Muslim Dalits. For the current version of the President's Constitution (Scheduled Castes) Order, which tells us who will count as SC for the purposes of constitutional and legal protections, is entirely unambiguous: "No person who professes a religion different from the Hindu, the Sikh or the Buddhist religion shall be deemed to be a member of a Scheduled Caste". She goes on to say, "It was only under Congress rule, in 1950, that the President's Order explicitly defined SC on the basis of religious criteria, although Christian Dalits were excluded from SC for electoral purposes by the Government of India Act 1935. From that point onwards, Dalits who had converted out of Hinduism lost not only reservations, but also, after 1989, protection under the Prevention of Atrocities Act. Later, SC was expanded to include Sikh and Buddhist Dalits, but official discrimination against Muslim and Christian Dalits remains". If Christians as well as Muslims who face the stigma of caste were to be included in the number of those who can be counted as Dalit, their share in the Indian population would far exceed the official 2011 Census figure of 17 per cent. See also Note 2 to the Preface of the 1937 edition of AoC (184).

7   On 16 December 2012, a woman was brutally tortured and gang-raped in a bus in New Delhi. She died on 29 December. The atrocity led to mass protests for days together. Unusually, a large number of middle-class people participated in them. In the wake of the protests the law against rape was made more stringent. See Jason Burke's reports in *The Guardian*, especially "Delhi Rape: How India's Other Half Lives" (10 September 2013). http://www.theguardian.com/world/2013/sep/10/delhi-gang-rape-india-women. Accessed 12 September 2013.

8   National Crime Records Bureau (NCRB) 2012, 423–4.

9   Privileged castes punish Dalits by forcing them to eat human excreta though this often goes unreported. In Thinniyam village in Tamil Nadu's Tiruchi district, on 22 May 2002, two Dalits, Murugesan and Ramasami, were forced to feed each other human excreta and branded with hot iron rods for publicly declaring that they had been cheated by the village chief. See Viswanathan (2005). In fact, "The Statement of Objects and Reasons of the Scheduled Castes and Scheduled Tribes (Prevention of Atrocities) Act, 1989" states this

as one of the crimes it seeks to redress: "Of late, there has been an increase in the disturbing trend of commission of certain atrocities like making the Scheduled Caste person eat inedible substances like human excreta and attacks on and mass killings of helpless Scheduled Castes and Scheduled Tribes and rape of women belonging to the Scheduled Castes and Scheduled Tribes".

10 According to the tenets of their faith, Sikhs are not supposed to practise caste. However, those from the Untouchable castes who converted to Sikhism continue to be treated as Untouchable. For an account of how caste affects Sikhism, see Mark Juergensmeyer (1982/2009).

11 BAWS 1, 222.

12 See, for example, Madhu Kishwar (*Tehelka*, 11 February 2006) who says "the much reviled caste system has played a very significant role in making Indian democracy vibrant by making it possible for people to offer a good measure of resistance to centralised, authoritarian power structures that came to be imposed during colonial rule and were preserved even after Independence".

13 See Béteille (2001) and Gupta (2001, 2007). Dipankar Gupta, formerly professor of sociology at Jawaharlal Nehru University, was part of the official Indian delegation that in 2007 opposed the Dalit caucus's demand to treat caste discrimination as being akin to racial discrimination. In an essay in 2007, Gupta argued that "the allegation that caste is a form of racial discrimination is not just an academic misjudgement but has unfortunate policy consequences as well". For a cross-section of views on the caste–race debate at the United Nations Committee on Elimination of Racial Discrimination, see Thorat and Umakant (ed., 2004), which features counter-arguments by a range of scholars including Gail Omvedt and Kancha Ilaiah. Also see Natarajan and Greenough (ed., 2009).

14 For a response to Béteille and Gupta, see Gerald D. Berreman in Natarajan and Greenough (2009). Berreman says: "What is 'scientifically nonsensical' is Professor Béteille's misunderstanding of 'race'. What is 'mischievous' is his insistence that India's system of ascribed social inequality should be exempted from the provisions of a UN Convention whose sole purpose is the extension of human rights to include freedom from all forms of discrimination and intolerance—and to which India, along with most other nations, has committed itself" (54–5).

15 See www.declarationofempathy.org. Accessed 16 January 2014.

16 Das 2010, 25.

17 Inter-caste and intra-gotra marriages are resisted in the name of 'honour'; in extreme cases, the couple, or one of the partners, is killed. For an account of the case of Ilavarasan and Divya from

Tamil Nadu, see Meena Kandasamy (2013). For an account of the consequences of violating 'gotra laws' in Haryana, see Chander Suta Dogra's recent *Manoj and Babli: A Hate Story* (2013). Also see "Day after Their Killing, Village Goes Quiet", *Indian Express*, 20 September 2013, and Chowdhry (2007).

18   In 2009, Ahmedabad-based Navsarjan Trust and the Robert F. Kennedy Center for Justice and Human Rights published a joint report, "Understanding Untouchability". It listed ninety-nine forms of untouchability in 1,589 villages of Gujarat. It looked at the prevalence of untouchability under eight broad heads: 1. Water for Drinking; 2. Food and Beverage; 3. Religion; 4. Caste-based Occupations; 5. Touch; 6. Access to Public Facilities and Institutions; 7. Prohibitions and Social Sanctions; 8. Private Sector Discrimination. The findings were shocking. In 98.4 per cent of villages surveyed, inter-caste marriage was prohibited; in 97.6 per cent of villages, Dalits were forbidden to touch water pots or utensils that belonged to non-Dalits; in 98.1 per cent of villages, a Dalit could not rent a house in a non-Dalit area; in 97.2 per cent of villages, Dalit religious leaders were not allowed to celebrate a religious ceremony in a non-Dalit area; in 67 per cent of villages, Dalit panchayat members were either not offered tea or were served in separate cups called 'Dalit' cups.

19   AoC 17.7.

20   CWMG 15, 160–1. All references to Gandhi's works, unless otherwise stated, are from *The Collected Works of Mahatma Gandhi* (CWMG) (1999). Wherever possible, first publication details are also provided since scholars sometimes refer to an earlier edition of the CWMG.

21   Cited in BAWS 9, 276.

22   Cited in CWMG 59, 227.

23   See the 20 November 2009 UNI report, "India's 100 Richest Are 25 Pc of GDP". http://ibnlive.in.com/news/indias-100-richest-are-25-pc-of-gdp-forbes/105548-7.html?utm_source=ref_article. Accessed 8 September 2013.

24   A Reuters report (10 August 2007) based on "Conditions of Work and Promotions of Livelihoods in the Unorganised Sector" by the National Commission for Enterprises in the Unorganised Sector said: "Seventy-seven per cent of Indians—about 836 million people—live on less than half a dollar a day in one of the world's hottest economies". http://in.reuters.com/article/2007/08/10/idIN   India-28923020070810. Accessed 26 August 2013.

25   S. Gurumurthy, co-convenor of the Hindu right-wing Swadeshi Jagaran Manch, talks of how caste and capitalism can coexist: "Caste is a very strong bond. While individuals are related by families, castes link the families. Castes transcended the local limits and

networked the people across [sic]. This has prevented the disturbance that industrialism caused to neighbourhood societies in the West, resulting in unbridled individualism and acute atomization." He goes on to argue that the caste system "has in modern times engaged the market in economics and democracy in politics to reinvent itself. It has become a great source of entrepreneurship". See "Is Caste an Economic Development Vehicle?", *The Hindu*, 19 January 2009. http://www.hindu.com/2009/01/19/stories/2009011955440900. htm. Accessed 26 August 2013.

26 See "Forbes: India's Billionaire Wealth Much above Country's Fiscal Deficit", *The Indian Express*, 5 March 2013. http://www.indianexpress. com/news/forbes-indias-billionaire-wealth-much-above-countrys-fiscal-deficit/1083500/#sthash.KabcY8BJ.dpuf. Accessed 26 August 2013.

27 Hutton 1935.

28 Hardiman 1996, 15.

29 See "Brahmins in India", *Outlook*, 4 June 2007. http://www. outlookindia.com/article.aspx?234783. Accessed 5 September 2013. Despite the decline, the Lok Sabha in 2007 had fifty Brahmin Members of Parliament—9.17 per cent of the total strength of the House. The data given by *Outlook* is based on four surveys conducted by the Centre for the Study of Developing Societies, Delhi, between 2004 and 2007.

30 BAWS 9, 207.

31 See Singh 1990. Singh's figures are based on information provided by one of his readers.

32 BAWS 9, 200.

33 Reservation was first introduced in India during the colonial period. For a history of the policy of reservation, see Bhagwan Das (2000).

34 *Selected Educational Statistics 2004–05*, p.xxii, Ministry of Human Resource Development. Available at http://www.education-forallinindia.com/SES2004-05.pdf. Accessed 11 November 2013.

35 Under the new economic regime, education, health care, essential services and other public institutions are rapidly being privatised. It has led to a haemorrhage of government jobs. For a population of 1.2 billion people, the total number of organised sector jobs is 29 million (as of 2011). Of these, the private sector accounts for only 11.4 million. See the *Economic Survey 2010–11*, p.A52. http:// indiabudget.nic.in/budget2011-2012/es2010-11/estat1.pdf. Accessed 10 November 2013.

36 See Ajay Navaria's story "Yes Sir" in *Unclaimed Terrain* (2013).

37 National Commission for Scheduled Castes and Scheduled Tribes (NCSCST) 1998, 180–1.

38 Prabhu Chawla, "Courting Controversy", *India Today* (29 January

1999). The lawyers quoted are Anil Divan and Fali S. Nariman. Later, India did get a Dalit Supreme Court Chief Justice in K.G. Balakrishnan (2007–10).

39   Santhosh and Abraham 2010, 28.

40   Ibid., 27.

41   The note submitted to the JNU vice-chancellor was signed by, among others, Yoginder K. Alagh, T.K. Oommen and Bipan Chandra. Alagh is an economist and a former Member of Parliament (Rajya Sabha), a former union minister and regular newspaper columnist. Oomen was president of the International Sociological Association (1990–4), and published an edited volume called *Classes, Citizenship and Inequality: Emerging Perspectives*. Chandra is a Marxist historian, former president of the Indian History Congress, and was chairperson of the Centre for Historical Studies, JNU.

42   Raman 2010.

43   The Justice Rajinder Sachar Committee was appointed by Prime Minister Manmohan Singh on 9 March 2005 to assess the social, economic and educational status of the Muslim community of India; its 403-page report was tabled in Parliament on 30 November 2006. The report establishes that caste oppression affects India's Muslims too. According to Teltumbde (2010a, 16), "working from the Sachar Committee data, the SC and ST components of India's population can be estimated at 19.7 and 8.5 per cent respectively".

44   According to economist Sukhadeo Thorat (2009, 56), "Nearly 70 per cent of SC households either do not own land or have very small landholdings of less than 0.4 ha [hectare]. A very small proportion (less than 6 per cent) consists of medium and large farmers. The scenario of landownership among SCs is even grimmer in Bihar, Haryana, Kerala and Punjab, where more than 90 per cent of SC households possess negligible or no land." Citing Planning Commission data, another research paper states that the majority of the Scheduled Castes (77 per cent) are landless, without any productive assets and sustainable employment opportunities. According to the Agricultural Census of 1990–1, the essay says, "Around 87 per cent of the landholders of scheduled castes and 65 per cent of scheduled tribes in the country belong to the category of small and marginal farmers" (Mohanty 2001, 3857).

45   NCSCST 1998, 176.

46   "13 Lakh Dalits Still Engaged in Manual Scavenging: Thorat", *The New Indian Express*, 8 October 2013. See http://www.newindianexpress.com/cities/hyderabad/13-lakh-Dalits-still-engaged-in-manual-scavenging-Thorat/2013/10/08/article1824760.ece. Accessed 10 October 2013. See also the status papers on the website of the International Dalit Solidarity Network, http://idsn.org/caste-discrimination/key-issues/

manual-scavenging/. Accessed 10 October 2013.

47   Data   from   http://www.indianrailways.gov.in/railwayboard/
      uploads/directorate/stat_econ/pdf/Summarypercent20Sheet_Eng.
      pdf accessed 26 August 2013, and Bhasin (2013).

48   See the interview of Milind Kamble, chairman of DICCI, and
      Chandra Bhan Prasad, mentor to DICCI, in *The Indian Express*,
      11 June 2013: "Capitalism is changing caste much faster than any
      human being. Dalits should look at capitalism as a crusader against
      caste." Available at http://m.indianexpress.com/news/capitalism-is-
      changing-caste-much-faster-than-any-human-being.-dalits-should-
      look-at-capitalism-as-a-crusader-against-caste/1127570/.   Accessed
      20 August 2013. For an analysis of how India's policies of liberalisation
      and globalisation since 1990 have actually benefited rural Dalits of
      Uttar Pradesh's Azamgarh and Bulandshahar districts, see Kapur, et
      al. (2010). See also Milind Khandekar's *Dalit Millionaires: 15 Inspiring
      Stories* (2013). For a critique of the "low-intensity spectacle of Dalit
      millionaires", see Gopal Guru (2012).

49   "Anti-caste Discrimination Reforms Blocked, Say Critics", *The
      Guardian*, 29 July 2013. See http://www.theguardian.com/uk-
      news/2013/jul/29/anticaste-discrimination-reforms.   Accessed   5
      August 2013.

50   Vanita 2002.

51   Sukta 90 in Book X of the *Rig Veda* tells the story of the myth of
      creation. It describes the sacrifice of the Purusha (primeval man),
      from whose body the four varnas and the entire universe emerged.
      When (the gods) divided the Purusha, his mouth became Brahmin,
      his arms Kshatriya, his thighs Vaishya, and Shudra sprang from his
      feet. See Doniger (translation, 2005). Some scholars believe that
      Sukta is a latter-day interpolation into the *Rig Veda*.

52   Susan Bayly (1998) shows how Gandhi's caste politics are completely
      in keeping with the views of modern, privileged-caste Hindu
      'reformers'.

53   In 2012, the newsmagazine *Outlook* published the result of just such
      a poll conducted on the eve of independence day. The question
      was: "Who, after the Mahatma, is the greatest Indian to have walked
      our soil?" Ambedkar topped the poll and *Outlook* devoted an entire
      issue (20 August 2012) to him. See http://www.outlookindia.com/
      content10894.asp. Accessed 10 August 2013.

54   See Ambedkar's *Pakistan or the Partition of India* (1945), first published
      as *Thoughts on Pakistan* (1940), and featured now in BAWS 8.

55   Parel 1997, 188–9.

56   In a 1955 interview with BBC radio, Ambedkar says: "A comparative
      study of Gandhi's Gujarati and English writings will reveal how
      Mr Gandhi was deceiving people". See http://www.youtube.com/

watch?v=ZJs-BjoSzbo. Accessed 12 August 2013.

57   Cited in BAWS 9, 276.

58   AoC 16.2.

59   See Tidrick 2006, 281, 283–4. On 2 May 1938, after Gandhi had a seminal discharge at the age of sixty-four, in a letter to Amritlal Nanavati he said: "Where is my place, and how can a person subject to passion represent non-violence and truth?" (CWMG 73, 139).

60   BAWS 9, 202.

61   Keer 1954/1990, 167.

62   For an analysis of the radicalism inherent in the Ambedkar statue, in the context of Uttar Pradesh, see Nicolas Jaoul (2006). "To Dalit villagers, whose rights and dignity have been regularly violated, setting up the statue of a Dalit statesman wearing a red tie and carrying the Constitution involves dignity, pride in emancipated citizenship and a practical acknowledgement of the extent to which the enforcement of laws could positively change their lives" (204).

63   "The State represents violence in a concentrated and organised form. The individual has a soul, but as the State is a soulless machine, it can never be weaned from violence to which it owes its very existence. Hence I prefer the doctrine of trusteeship". *Hindustan Times*, 17 October 1935; CWMG 65, 318.

64   *Young India*, 16 April 1931; CWMG 51, 354.

65   Das 2010, 175.

66   Jefferson says this in his letter of 6 September 1789 to James Madison. Available at http://press-pubs.uchicago.edu/founders/documents/v1ch2s23.html. Accessed 21 November 2013.

67   Ambedkar argues in "Castes in India", his 1916 essay, that women are the gateways of the caste system and that control over them through child marriages, enforced widowhood and sati (being burnt on a dead husband's pyre) are methods to keep a check on women's sexuality. For an analysis of Ambedkar's writings on this issue, see Sharmila Rege (2013).

68   For a discussion of the Hindu Code Bill, its ramifications and how it was sabotaged, see Sharmila Rege (2013, 191–244). Rege shows how from 11 April 1947, when it was introduced in the Constituent Assembly, till September 1951, the Bill was never taken seriously. Ambedkar finally resigned on 10 October 1951. The Hindu Marriage Act was finally enacted in 1955, granting divorce rights to Hindu women. The Special Marriage Act, passed in 1954 allows inter-caste and inter-religious marriage.

69   Rege 2013, 200.

70   Rege 2013, 241. Ambedkar's disillusionment with the new legal regime in India went further. On 2 September 1953, Ambedkar declared in the Rajya Sabha, "Sir, my friends tell me that I made the Constitution.

But I am quite prepared to say that I shall be the first person to burn it out. I do not want it. It does not suit anybody. But whatever that may be, if our people want to carry on, they must remember that there are majorities and there are minorities; and they simply cannot ignore the minorities by saying: 'Oh, no, to recognise you is to harm democracy'" (Keer 1990, 499).

71 AoC 20.12.
72 Omvedt 2008, 19.
73 Unpublished translation by Joel Lee, made available through personal communication.
74 *Young India*, 17 March 1927; CWMG 38, 210.
75 Ambedkar said this during his speech delivered as Chairman of the Constitution Drafting Committee in the Constituent Assembly on 4 November 1948. See Das 2010, 176.
76 For an analysis of Gandhi's relationship with Indian capitalists, see Leah Renold (1994). Gandhi's approach to big dams is revealed in a letter dated 5 April 1924, in which he advised villagers who faced displacement by the Mulshi Dam, being built by the Tatas to generate electricity for their Bombay mills, to give up their protest (CWMG 27, 168):

   1. I understand that the vast majority of the men affected have accepted compensation and that the few who have not cannot perhaps even be traced.
   2. The dam is nearly half-finished and its progress cannot be permanently stopped. There seems to me to be no ideal behind the movement.
   3. The leader of the movement is not a believer out and out in non-violence. This defect is fatal to success.

   Seventy-five years later, in 2000, the Supreme Court of India used very similar logic in its infamous judgement on the World Bank-funded Sardar Sarovar Dam on the Narmada river, when it ruled against tens of thousands of local people protesting their displacement, and ordered the construction of the dam to continue.
77 *Young India*, 20 December 1928; CWMG 43, 412. Also see Gandhi's *Hind Swaraj* (1909) in Anthony Parel (1997).
78 Rege 2013, 100.
79 BAWS 5, 102.
80 In Das 2010, 51.
81 AoC, Preface to 1937 edition.
82 Cited in Zelliot 2013, 147.
83 Here, for example, is Ismat Chugtai, a Muslim writer celebrated for her progressive, feminist views, describing an Untouchable sweeper in her short story, "A Pair of Hands": "Gori was her name, the feckless one, and she was dark, dark like a glistening pan on which a roti had been fried but which a careless cook had forgotten to clean. She had a bulbous nose, a wide jaw, and it seemed she came from a family

where brushing one's teeth was a habit long forgotten. The squint in her left eye was noticeable despite the fact that her eyes were heavily kohled; it was difficult to imagine how, with a squinted eye, she was able to throw darts that never failed to hit their mark. Her waist was not slim; it had thickened, rapidly increasing in diameter from all those handouts she consumed. There was also nothing delicate about her feet which reminded one of a cow's hoofs, and she left a coarse smell of mustard oil in her wake. Her voice however, was sweet" (2003, 164).

84   In 1981, all the Dalits of the village of Meenakshipuram—renamed Rahmat Nagar—in Tamil Nadu's Tirunelveli district converted to Islam. Worried by this, Hindu supremacist groups such as the Vishwa Hindu Parishad and the Rashtriya Swayamsevak Sangh together with the Sankaracharya of Kanchipuram began to work proactively to 'integrate' Dalits into Hinduism. A new 'Tamil Hindu' chauvinist group called the Hindu Munnani was formed. Eighteen years later, P. Sainath revisited Meenakshipuram and filed two reports (1999a, 1999b). For a similar case from Koothirambakkam, another village in Tamil Nadu, see S. Anand (2002).

85   Cited in Omvedt 2008, 177.

86   The figure Ambedkar cites is drawn from the Simon Commission report of 1930. When the Lothian Committee came to India in 1932 Ambedkar said, "The Hindus adopted a challenging mood and refused to accept the figures given by the Simon Commission as a true figure for the Untouchables of India". He then argues that "this is due to the fact that the Hindus had by now realised the danger of admitting the existence of the Untouchables. For it meant that a part of the representation enjoyed by the Hindus will have to be given up by them to the Untouchables" (BAWS 5, 7–8).

87   See Note 69 at 9.4 of this AoC edition.

88   He says this in the April 1899 issue of the journal *Prabuddha Bharata*, in an interview to its editor. In the same interview, when asked specifically what would be the caste of those who "re-converted" to Hinduism, Vivekananda says: "Returning converts ... will gain their own castes, of course. And new people will make theirs. You will remember ... that this has already been done in the case of Vaishnavism. Converts from different castes and aliens were all able to combine under that flag and form a caste by themselves—and a very respectable one too. From Ramanuja down to Chaitanya of Bengal, all great Vaishnava Teachers have done the same." Available at http://www. ramakrishnavivekananda.info/vivekanandavolume_5/interviews /on_the_bounds_of_hinduism.htm. Accessed 20 August 2013.

89   The names of these organisations translate as: Forum for Dalit Uplift; the All-India Committee for the Uplift of Untouchables; the Punjab Society for Untouchable Uplift.

90 AoC 6.2.
91 Bayly 1998.
92 The term was coined by V.D. Savarkar (1883–1966), one of the principal proponents of modern, right-wing Hindu nationalism, in his 1923 pamphlet *Essentials of Hindutva* (later retitled *Hindutva: Who Is a Hindu?*). The first edition (1923) of this work carried the pseudonymous "A Maratha" as author. For a critical introduction to Hindutva, see Jyotirmaya Sharma (2006).
93 Cited in Prashad 1996, 554–5.
94 BAWS 9, 195.
95 A few privileged-caste Hindu members of the Ghadar Party later turned towards Hindu nationalism and became Vedic missionaries. On Bhai Parmanand, a founder-member of the Ghadar Party who later became a Hindutva ideologue, see Note 11 in the Prologue to AoC.
96 For a monograph on the Ad Dharm movement, see Juergensmeyer (1982/2009).
97 Viswanath 2014 details the history of the colonial state's alliance with the landed castes against landless Dalits in the context of the Madras Presidency.
98 Davis 2002, 7.
99 BAWS 9, 1.
100 Ibid., 3.
101 See Devji 2012, chapter 3, "In Praise of Prejudice", especially 47–8.
102 Cited from *Young India*, 23 March 1921, in Devji 2012, 81.
103 Golwalkar 1945, 55–6.
104 BAWS 17, Part 1, 369–75.
105 Godse 1998, 43.
106 BAWS 3, 360.
107 Cited in BAWS 9, 68.
108 *Harijan*, 30 September 1939; CWMG 76, 356.
109 See Guha 2013b.
110 Tidrick 2006, 106.
111 For an archive of Gandhi's writings about his years in South Africa (1893 to 1914), see G.B. Singh (2004).
112 Swan 1985, 52.
113 Kaffir is an Arabic term that originally meant 'one who hides or covers'—a description of farmers burying seeds in the ground. After the advent of Islam, it came to mean 'non-believers' or 'heretics', those 'who covered the truth (Islam)'. It was first applied to non-Muslim Black people encountered by Arab traders along the Swahili coast. Portuguese explorers adopted the term and passed it on to the British, French and Dutch. In South Africa, it became a racial slur the Whites and Afrikaners (and Indians like Gandhi) used to describe

native Africans. Today, to call someone a Kaffir in South Africa is an actionable offence.

114 CWMG 1, 192–3.

115 CWMG 1, 200.

116 For a history of indentured labour in South Africa, see Ashwin Desai and Goolam Vahed (2010).

117 Between the early 1890s and 1913, the Indian population in South Africa tripled, from 40,000 to 135,000 (Guha 2013b, 463).

118 Guha 2013b, 115.

119 CWMG 2, 6.

120 Hochschild 2011, 33–4.

121 During the Second World War, he advised the Jews to "summon to their aid the soul-power that comes only from non-violence" and assured them that Herr Hitler would "bow before their courage" (*Harijan*, 17 December 1938; CWMG 74, 298). He urged the British to "fight Nazism without arms" (*Harijan*, 6 July 1940; CWMG 78, 387).

122 CWMG 34, 18.

123 CWMG 2, 339–40.

124 *The Natal Advertiser*, 16 October 1901; CWMG 2, 421.

125 CWMG 5, 11.

126 Ibid., 179.

127 Guy 2005, 212.

128 According to a note on the first page of volume 34 of CWMG, "Gandhiji started writing in Gujarati the history of Satyagraha in South Africa on November 26, 1923, when he was in the Yeravada Central Jail; vide Jail Diary, 1923. By the time he was released, on February 5, 1924, he had completed 30 chapters… The English translation by Valji G. Desai, which was seen and approved by Gandhiji, was published by S. Ganesan, Madras, in 1928".

129 CWMG 34, 82–3.

130 Ibid., 84.

131 Of a total population of 135,000 Indians, only 10,000, who were mostly traders, lived in the Transvaal. The rest were based in Natal (Guha 2013b, 463).

132 CWMG 5, 337. This is from Clause 3 from Resolution 2 of the Five Resolutions passed by the British Indian Association in Johannesburg, following the 'Mass Meeting' of 11 September 1906.

133 *Indian Opinion*, 7 March 1908; CWMG 8, 198–9.

134 CWMG 9, 256–7.

135 *Indian Opinion*, 23 January 1909; CWMG 9, 274.

136 In a letter dated 18 May 1899 to the Colonial Secretary, Gandhi wrote: "An Indian may fancy that he has a wrong to be redressed in that he does not get ghee instead of oil" (CWMG 2, 266). On

another occasion: "The regulations here do not provide for any ghee or fat to Indians. A complaint has therefore been made to the physician, and he has promised to look into it. So there is reason to hope that the inclusion of ghee will be ordered" (*Indian Opinion*, 17 October 1908; CWMG 9, 197).

137 *Indian Opinion*, 23 January 1909; CWMG 9, 270.

138 *Young India*, 5 April 1928; CWMG 41, 365.

139 Lelyveld 2011, 74.

140 Cited in Zinn and Arnove 2004, 265.

141 Ibid., 270.

142 Cited in Omvedt 2008, 219.

143 In Deshpande 2002, 25.

144 Ibid., 38–40.

145 Cited in Ambedkar 1945; BAWS 9, 276.

146 See Adams 2011, 263–5. Also see Rita Banerji 2008, especially 265–81.

147 CWMG 34, 201–2.

148 *Hind Swaraj* in Parel 1997, 106.

149 Ibid., 97

150 See Gandhi's Preface to the English translation of *Hind Swaraj*, in Parel (1997, 5).

151 Savarkar, the militant Hindutva ideologue, said a true Indian is one whose *pitrabhoomi* (fatherland) as well as *punyabhoomi* (holy land) is India—not some foreign land. See his *Hindutva* (1923, 105).

152 Parel 1997, 47–51.

153 Ibid., 66.

154 Ibid., 68–9.

155 Ramachandra Guha (2013b, 383) says: "Gandhi wrote *Hind Swaraj* in 1909 at a time he scarcely knew India at all. By 1888, when he departed for London, at the age of nineteen, he had lived only in towns in his native Kathiawar. There is no evidence that he had travelled in the countryside, and he knew no other part of India".

156 Parel 1997, 69–70.

157 Gandhi says this in 1932, in connection with the debate around separate electorates for Untouchables, in a letter to Sir Samuel Hoare, Secretary of State for India. Cited in BAWS 9, 78.

158 *Indian Opinion*, 22 October 1910; CWMG 11, 143–4. Cited also in Guha 2013b, 395.

159 Guha 2013b, 463.

160 Ibid., 406.

161 Aiyar quoted in Lelyveld 2011, 21.

162 Personal communication, Ashwin Desai, professor of sociology at University of Johannesburg.

163 Lelyveld 2011, 130.

164 Tidrick 2006, 188.

165 See Renold 1994. Also see Louis Fischer, *A Week with Gandhi* (1942), quoted by Ambedkar: "'I said I had several questions to ask him about the Congress Party. Very highly placed Britishers, I recalled, had told me that Congress was in the hands of big business and that Gandhi was supported by the Bombay Mill-owners who gave him as much money as he wanted. 'What Truth is there in these assertions', I asked. 'Unfortunately, they are true,' he declared simply … 'What portion of the Congress budget,' I asked, 'is covered by rich Indians?' 'Practically all of it,' he stated. 'In this ashram, for instance, we could live much more poorly than we do and spend less money. But we do not and the money comes from our rich friends'". Cited in BAWS 9, 208.

166 Cited in Amin 1998, 293.

167 *Young India*, 18 August 1921; CWMG 23, 158.

168 *Harijan*, 25 August 1940; CWMG 79, 133–4.

169 Ibid., 135.

170 Ibid., 135.

171 *The Gospel of Wealth* (1889). Available at http://www.swarthmore.edu/SocSci/rbannis1/AIH19th/Carnegie.html. Accessed 26 August 2013.

172 Cited in Amin 1998, 290–1.

173 Amin 291–2.

174 Tidrick 2006, 191.

175 Cited in Singh 2004, 124.

176 Tidrick 2006, 192.

177 Ibid., 194.

178 Ibid., 195.

179 Zelliot 2013, 48.

180 This is from the unpublished preface to Ambedkar's *The Buddha and His Dhamma* (1956). It first appeared as part of a book of Ambedkar's prefaces, published by Bhagwan Das and entitled *Rare Prefaces* (1980). Eleanor Zelliot later published it on the Columbia University website dedicated to Ambedkar's life and selected works. http://www.columbia.edu/itc/mealac/pritchett/00ambedkar/ambedkar_buddha/00_pref_unpub.html. Accessed 10 September 2013.

181 BAWS 4, 1986.

182 On 20 May 1857, the Education Department issued a directive that "no boy be refused admission to a government college or school merely on the ground of caste" (Nambissan 2002, 81).

183 For an annotated edition of this essay, see Sharmila Rege (2013). It also appears in BAWS 1.

184 In *Autobiographical Notes* 2003, 19.

185 Keer 1990, 36–7.

186 AoC 17.5.

187 Prashad 1996, 552. In his speech at the Suppressed Classes Conference in Ahmedabad on 13 April 1921, reported in *Young India* on 27 April 1921 and 4 May 1921 (reproduced in CWMG 23, 41–7), Gandhi discussed Uka at length for the first time (42). Bakha, the main protagonist in Mulk Raj Anand's iconic novel *Untouchable* (1935), is said to be inspired by Uka. According to the researcher Lingaraja Gandhi (2004), Anand showed his manuscript to Gandhi, who suggested changes. Anand says: "I read my novel to Gandhiji, and he suggested that I should cut down more than a hundred pages, especially those passages in which Bakha seemed to be thinking and dreaming and brooding like a Bloomsbury intellectual". Lingaraja Gandhi further says: "Anand had provided long and flowery speeches to Bakha in his draft. Gandhi instructed Anand that untouchables don't speak that way: in fact, they hardly speak. The novel underwent metamorphosis under the tutelage of Gandhi".

188 *Navajivan*, 18 January 1925; CWMG 30, 71. In the account of Gandhi's secretary, Mahadev Desai, this speech from Gujarati is rendered differently: "The position that I really long for is that of the Bhangi. How sacred is this work of cleanliness! That work can be done only by a Brahmin or by a Bhangi. The Brahmin may do it in his wisdom, the Bhangi in ignorance. I respect, I adore both of them. If either of the two disappears from Hinduism, Hinduism itself would disappear. And it is because seva-dharma (self-service) is dear to my heart that the Bhangi is dear to me. I may even sit at my meals with a Bhangi by my side, but I do not ask you to align yourselves with them by inter-caste dinners and marriages". Cited in Ramaswamy 2005, 86.

189 Renold 1994, 19–20. Highly publicised symbolic visits to Dalit homes has become a Congress party tradition. In January 2009, in the glare of a media circus, the Congress party's vice-president and prime ministerial candidate, Rahul Gandhi, along with David Miliband, the British foreign secretary, spent a night in the hut of a Dalit family in Simra village of Uttar Pradesh. For an account of this, see Anand Teltumbde (2013).

190 Prashad 2001, 139.

191 BAWS 1, 256.

192 Keer 1990, 41.

193 Zelliot 2013, 91.

194 See Joseph 2003, 166. Objecting to Sikhs running a langar (free, common kitchen) for the satyagrahis of Vaikom, Gandhi wrote in *Young India* (8 May 1924), "The Vaikom satyagraha is, I fear, crossing the limits. I do hope that the Sikh free kitchen will be withdrawn and that the movement will be confined to Hindus only" (CWMG 27, 362).

195 Chakravarti Rajagopalachari, a Tamil Brahmin, known affectionately as Rajaji, was a close friend and confidant of Gandhi. In 1933, his daughter Leela married Gandhi's son Devdas. Rajagopalachari later served as the acting Governor General of India. In 1947, he became the first Governor of West Bengal, and in 1955 received the Bharat Ratna, India's highest civilian award.

196 Cited in Joseph 2003, 168.

197 *Young India*, 14 August 1924; CWMG 28, 486.

198 Joseph 2003, 169.

199 Birla 1953, 43.

200 Keer 1990, 79.

201 Speaking at a Depressed Classes Conference in 1925, Ambedkar said: "When one is spurned by everyone, even the sympathy shown by Mahatma Gandhi is of no little importance". Cited in Jaffrelot 2005, 63. Gandhi visited Mahad on 3 March 1927, a fortnight before the first satyagraha, but unlike at Vaikom he did not interfere. For an account of the second Mahad Satyagraha when a copy of the *Manusmriti* was burnt, see K. Jamnadas (2010).

202 According to Anand Teltumbde's unpublished manuscript on the two Mahad conferences, Resolution No. 2 seeking a 'ceremonial cremation' of the *Manusmriti* was proposed by G.N. Sahasrabuddhe, a Brahmin, who played an important role in the March events as well; it was seconded by P.N. Rajbhoj, a Chambhar leader. According to Teltumbde, "There was a deliberate attempt to get some progressive people from non-untouchable communities to the conference, but eventually only two names materialised. One was Gangadhar Nilkanth Sahasrabuddhe, an activist of the Social Service League and a leader of the cooperative movement belonging to Agarkari Brahman caste, and the other was Vinayak alias Bhai Chitre, a Chandraseniya Kayastha Prabhu". In the 1940s, Sahasrabuddhe became the editor of *Janata*—another of Ambedkar's newspapers.

203 Dangle, ed., 1992, 231–3.

204 Keer 1990, 170.

205 Cited in Prashad 1996, 555.

206 Gandhi outlined the difference between satyagraha and duragraha in a speech on 3 November 1917: "There are two methods of attaining one's goal: Satyagraha and Duragraha. In our scriptures, they have been described, respectively, as divine and devilish modes of action". He went on to give an example of duragraha: "the terrible War going on in Europe". Also, "The man who follows the path of Duragraha becomes impatient and wants to kill the so-called enemy. There can be but one result of this. Hatred increases" (CWMG 16, 126–8).

207 BAWS 9, 247.

208 On the fallout with the Girni Kamgar Union, see Teltumbde (2012).

For how Dange and the Communist Party worked towards ensuring Ambedkar's defeat in the Bombay City North constituency in the 1952 general election, see S. Anand (2012a), and Rajnarayan Chandavarkar (2009, 161), where he says: "The decision by the socialists and the communists not to forge an electoral pact, let alone join together to combine with Ambedkar's Scheduled Castes Federation, against the Congress lost them the Central Bombay seat. Dange, for the CPI, Asoka Mehta for the socialists and Ambedkar each stood separately and fell together. Significantly, Dange instructed his supporters to spoil their ballots in the reserved constituency for Central Bombay rather than vote for Ambedkar. Indeed, Ambedkar duly lost and attributed his defeat to the communist campaign. Although the communists could not win the Central Bombay seat, their influence in Girangaon, including its dalit voters, was sufficient to decisively influence the outcome. The election campaign created a lasting bitterness. As Dinoo Ranadive recalls, 'the differences between the dalits and the communists became so sharp that even today it has become difficult for the communists to appeal to the Republicans' or at any rate to some sections of dalit voters". Republicans here refers to the Republican Party of India (RPI) that Ambedkar had conceived of a short while before his death in December 1956. It came to be established only in September 1957 by his followers, but today there are over a dozen splintered factions of the RPI.

209 Kosambi 1948, 274.

210 For an account of this, see Jan Breman's *The Making and Unmaking of an Industrial Working Class* (2004), especially chapter 2, "The Formalization of Collective Action: Mahatma Gandhi as a Union Leader" (40–68).

211 Breman 2004, 57.

212 Shankerlal Banker cited in Breman (2004, 47).

213 Annual Report of the Textile Labour Union, 1925, cited in Breman (2004, 51).

214 *Navajivan*, 8 February 1920; cited in BAWS 9, 280.

215 *Harijan*, 21 April 1946; CWMG 90, 255–6.

216 AoC 3.10 and 3.11.

217 AoC 4.1, emphasis original.

218 Zelliot 2013, 178.

219 Namboodiripad 1986, 492, emphasis added.

220 The text of the manifesto is reproduced in Satyanarayana and Tharu (2013, 62).

221 For a critical piece on the NGO–Dalit movement interface that traces it to the history of colonial and missionary activity in India, see Teltumbde (2010b), where he argues: "Unsurprisingly, most Dalits in Indian NGOs are active at the field level. Dalit boys and girls appear to be doing social services for their communities,

which is what Ambedkar expected educated Dalits to do, and Dalit communities therefore perceive such workers quite favourably—more favourably, certainly, than Dalit politicians, who are often seen as engaged in mere rhetoric. The NGO sector has thus become a significant employer for many Dalits studying for their humanities degree, typically capped with a postgraduate degree in social work. Further, as the prospects of public-sector jobs have decreased since the government's neoliberal reforms of the mid-1980s and later, the promise of NGOs as employers assumed great importance".

222 For instance, see the list of NGOs that work with the multinational mining corporation Vedanta, under fire for land-grab and several violations against the environment and Adivasi rights, at http://www.vedantaaluminium.com/ngos-govt-bodies.htm. Accessed 20 November 2013.

223 Speech on 26 September 1896 at a public meeting in Bombay where he said he was representing the "100,000 British Indians at present residing in South Africa". See CWMG 1, 407.

224 AoC 8.2–4.

225 BAWS 1, 375.

226 AoC 5.8.

227 There are different aspects of the Constitution that govern the Adivasis of the heartland (the Fifth Schedule) and those of the Northeast of India (the Sixth Schedule). As the political scientist Uday Chandra points out in a recent paper (2013, 155), "The Fifth and Sixth Schedules of the Constitution perpetuate the languages and logics of the Partially and Wholly Excluded Areas defined in the Government of India Act (1935) and the Typically and Really Backward Tracts defined by the Government of India (1918)... In the Schedule V areas, dispersed across eastern, western, and central Indian states, state governors wield special powers to prohibit or modify central or state laws, to prohibit or regulate the transfer of land by or among tribals, to regulate commercial activities, particularly by non-tribals, and to constitute tribal advisory councils to supplement state legislatures. In principle, New Delhi also reserves the right to intervene directly in the administration of these Scheduled Areas by bypassing elected state and local governments. In the Schedule VI areas, dispersed across the seven northeastern states formed out of the colonial province of Assam, state governors preside over District and Regional Councils in Autonomous Districts and Regions to ensure that state and central laws do not impinge on these administrative zones of exception".

228 Cited in BAWS 9, 70.

229 BAWS 9, 42.

230 As prime minister of a non-Congress, Janata Dal–led coalition

government from December 1989 to November 1990, Vishwanath Pratap Singh (1931–2008) took the decision to implement the recommendations of the Mandal Commission, which fixed a quota for members of the Backward Classes in jobs in the public sector to redress caste discrimination. The Commission, named after B.P. Mandal, a parliamentarian who headed it, had been established in 1979 by another non-Congress (Janata Party) government, headed by Morarji Desai, but the recommendations of its 1980 report— which extended the scope of reservation in public sector employment beyond Dalits and Adivasis, and allocated 27 per cent to Other Backward Classes (OBCs)—had not been implemented for ten years. When it was implemented, the privileged castes took to the streets. They symbolically swept the streets, pretended to shine shoes and performed other 'polluting' tasks to suggest that instead of becoming doctors, engineers, lawyers or economists, the policy of reservation was now going to reduce privileged castes to doing menial tasks. A few people attempted to publicly immolate themselves, the most well-known being a Delhi University student, Rajiv Goswami, in 1990. Similar protests were repeated in 2006 when the Congress-led United Progressive Alliance tried to extend reservation to the OBCs in institutes of higher education.

231 BAWS 9, 40.
232 See Menon 2003, 52–3.
233 In his 1945 indictment of the Congress and Gandhi, Ambedkar lists the names of these mock candidates in his footnotes: Guru Gosain Agamdas and Babraj Jaiwar were the two cobblers; Chunnu was the milkman; Arjun Lal the barber; Bansi Lal Chaudhari the sweeper (BAWS 9, 210).
234 BAWS 9, 210.
235 Ibid., 68.
236 Ibid., 69.
237 Tidrick 2006, 255.
238 Servants of India Society member Kodanda Rao's account cited in Jaffrelot (2005, 66).
239 In Pyarelal 1932, 188.
240 BAWS 9, 259.
241 As Ambedkar saw it, "The increase in the number of seats for the Untouchables is no increase at all and was no recompense for the loss of separate electorates and the double vote" (BAWS 9, 90). Ambedkar himself lost twice in the polls in post-1947 India. It took more than half a century for Kanshi Ram, the founder of a predominantly Dalit party, the Bahujan Samaj Party, and his protégé Mayawati to succeed in a first-past-the-post parliamentary democracy. This happened *despite* the Poona Pact. Kanshi Ram worked for years, painstakingly

making alliances with other subordinated castes to achieve this victory. To succeed in the elections, the BSP needed the peculiar demography of Uttar Pradesh and the support of many OBCs. For a Dalit candidate to win an election from an open seat—even in Uttar Pradesh—continues to be almost impossible.

242 See Alexander 2010.

243 Fischer 1951, 400–03.

244 Eleanor Zelliot writes, "Ambedkar had written the *manpatra* (welcome address, or literally, letter of honor) for Baloo Babaji Palwankar, known as P. Baloo, upon his return from a cricket tour in England nearly twenty years earlier, and had had some part in P. Balu's selection as a Depressed Class nominee on the Bombay Municipal Corporation in the early 1920s" (2013, 254). Baloo supported Gandhi during the Round Table Conferences and supported the Hindu Mahasabha position. Soon after the Poona Pact, in October 1933, Baloo contested as a Hindu Mahasabha candidate for the Bombay Municipality, but lost. In 1937, the Congress, in an effort to split the Untouchable vote, pitted Baloo, a Chambhar, against Ambedkar, a Mahar, who contested on the Independent Labour Party ticket, for a Bombay (East) 'reserved' seat in the Bombay Legislative Assembly. Ambedkar won narrowly.

245 For an outline of Rajah's career and how he came around to supporting Ambedkar in 1938 and 1942, see Note 5 at 1.5 of "A Vindication of Caste by Mahatma Gandhi" in AoC.

246 The Gujarat Freedom of Religion Act, 2003, makes it mandatory for a person who wants to convert into another religion to seek prior permission from a district magistrate. The text of the Act is available at http://www.lawsofindia.org/statelaw/2224/TheGujaratFreedomofReligionAct2003.html. An amendment bill to the Act was sent back to the Legislative Assembly by the then Gujarat Governor, Nawal Kishore Sharma, for reconsideration. It was subsequently dropped by the state government. One of the provisions in the amendment bill sought to clarify that Jains and Buddhists were to be construed as denominations of Hinduism. The Governor said that the amendment would be in violation of Article 25 of the Indian Constitution. See http://www.indianexpress.com/news/gujarat-withdraws-freedom-of-religion-amendment-bill/282818/1. To watch a video of Modi invoking M.K. Gandhi against conversion, see http://ibnlive.in.com/news/modi-quotes-mahatma-flays-religious-conversion/75119-3.html. Also see http://www.youtube.com/watch?v=wr6q1drP558. The Gujarat Animal Preservation (Amendment) Act, 2011, makes "transport of animals for slaughter" a punishable offence, widening the ambit of the original Act, which bans cow-slaughter. The Amendment

Act has also augmented the punishment to seven years' rigorous imprisonment from the earlier six months. In 2012, Narendra Modi greeted Indians on Janmashtami (observed as Krishna's birthday) with the following words: "Mahatma Gandhi and Acharya Vinoba Bhave worked tirelessly for the protection of mother cow, but this Government abandoned their teachings." See http://ibnlive.in.com/news/narendra-modi-rakes-up-cow-slaughter-issue-in-election-year-targets-congress/280876-37-64.html?utm_source=ref_article. (All internet links cited here were accessed 10 September 2013.) Gandhi said, "Anyone who is not ready to give his life to save the cow is not a Hindu" (interview to *Goseva* on 8 September 1933; CWMG 61, 372). Earlier, in 1924, he said, "When I see a cow, it is not an animal to eat, it is a poem of pity for me and I worship it and I shall defend its worship against the whole world" (reported in *Bombay Chronicle*, 30 December 1924; CWMG 29, 476).

247 See for instance, http://articles.timesofindia.indiatimes.com/keyword/mahatma-mandir. Accessed 20 December 2013.

248 For a history of the terms Harijan, Dalit and Scheduled Caste, see Note 8 to the Prologue of AoC.

249 BAWS 9, 126.

250 Ibid., 210.

251 Renold 1994, 25.

252 Tidrick 2006, 261.

253 BAWS 9, 125.

254 Ibid., 111.

255 Tharu and Lalita 1997, 215.

256 Ambedkar 2003, 25.

257 *Manusmriti* X: 123. See Doniger 1991.

258 *Harijan*, 28 November 1936; CWMG 70, 126–8.

259 Reported by the columnist Rajiv Shah in his *Times of India* blog of 1 December 2012, http://blogs.timesofindia.indiatimes.com/true-lies/entry/modi-s-spiritual-potion-to-woo-karmayogis. Shah says 5,000 copies of *Karmayogi* were printed with funding from the public sector unit, Gujarat State Petroleum Corporation, and that later he was told, by the Gujarat Information Department that it had, on instructions from Modi, withdrawn the book from circulation. Two years later, addressing 9,000-odd Safai Karmacharis (sanitation workers), Modi said, "A priest cleans a temple every day before prayers, you also clean the city like a temple. You and the temple priest work alike." See Shah's blog of 23 January 2013, http://blogs.timesofindia.indiatimes.com/true-lies/entry/modi-s-postal-ballot-confusion?sortBy=AGREE&th=1. Both accessed 12 November 2013.

260 CWMG 70, 76–7.

261 See "A Note on the Poona Pact" in Ambedkar, *Annihilation of Caste: The Annotated Critical Edition* (New York: Verso, 2014), 357–76.

262 Menon 2006, 20.

263 This assimilation finds its way into the Constitution. Explanation II of Article 25(2)(b) of the Constitution was the first time in independent India when the law categorised Buddhists, Sikhs and Jains as 'Hindu', even if 'only' for the purpose of "providing social welfare and reform or the throwing open of Hindu religious institutions of a public character to all classes and sections of Hindus". Later, codified Hindu personal law, like the Hindu Marriage Act, 1955, the Hindu Succession Act, 1956, etc., reinforced this position, as these statutes were applied to Buddhists, Sikhs and Jains. Pertinently, under Indian law an atheist is automatically classified as a Hindu. The judiciary has been sending out mixed signals, sometimes recognising the 'independent character' of these religions, and at other times, asserting that the "Sikhs and Jains, in fact, have throughout been treated as part of the wider Hindu community which has different sects, sub-sects, faiths, modes of worship and religious philosophies" (*Bal Patil & Anr* vs *Union Of India & Ors*, 8 August 2005). For Buddhists, Sikhs and Jains the struggle for recognition continues. There has been some success; for example, the Anand Marriage (Amendment) Act, 2012, freed Sikhs from the Hindu Marriage Act. On 20 January 2014, the Union Cabinet approved the notification of Jains as a minority community at the national level. Also see Note 246 on the Gujarat Freedom of Religion Act.

264 See Guha 2013a.

265 While NGOs and news reports suggest a toll of two thousand persons (see "A Decade of Shame" by Anupama Katakam, *Frontline*, 9 March 2012), then Union Minister of State for Home, Shriprakash Jaiswal (of the Congress party), told Parliament on 11 May 2005 that 790 Muslims and 254 Hindus were killed in the riots; 2,548 were injured and 223 persons were missing. See "Gujarat riot death toll revealed", http://news.bbc.co.uk/2/hi/south_asia/4536199.stm. Accessed 10 November 2013.

266 "Peoples Tribunal Highlights Misuse of POTA", *The Hindu*, 18 March 2004. See also "Human Rights Watch asks Centre to Repeal POTA", Press Trust of India, 8 September 2002.

267 See "Blood Under Saffron: The Myth of Dalit-Muslim Confrontation," *Round Table India*, 23 July 2013. http://goo.gl/7DU9uH. Accessed 10 September 2013.

268 See http://blogs.reuters.com/india/2013/07/12/interview-with-bjp-leader-narendra-modi/. Accessed 8 September 2013.

269 See "Dalit Leader Buries the Hatchet with RSS", *Times of India*, 31 August 2006. http://articles.timesofindia.indiatimes.com/2006-

08-31/india/27792531_1_rss-chief-k-sudarshan-rashtriya-swayamsevak-sangh-dalit-leader. Accessed 10 August 2013.

270 See Zelliot 2013, especially chapter 5, "Political Development, 1935–56". For an account of Jogendranath Mandal's life and work, see Dwaipayan Sen (2010).

271 PTI News Service, 20 March 1955, cited in Zelliot (2013, 193).

272 See Weiss, 2011.

273 For an account of how Ambedkar's Buddhism is an attempt to reconstruct the world, see Jondhale and Beltz (2004). For an alternative history of Buddhism in India, see Omvedt (2003).

274 BAWS 11, 322.

275 BAWS 17, Part 2, 444–5. On 14 September 1956, Ambedkar wrote a letter to Prime Minister Nehru. "The cost of printing is very heavy and will come to about Rs 20,000. This is beyond my capacity, and I am, therefore, canvassing help from all quarters. I wonder if the Government of India could purchase 500 copies for distribution among the various libraries and among the many scholars whom it is inviting during the course of this year for the celebration of Buddha's 2,500 years' anniversary." Nehru did not help him. The book was published posthumously.

276 Brahminic Hinduism believes in cosmic time that has neither beginning nor end, and alternates between cycles of creation and cessation. Each Mahayuga consists of four yuga—Krta or Satya Yuga (the golden age), followed by Treta, Dwapara and Kali. Each era, shorter than the previous one, is said to be more degenerate and depraved than the preceding one. In Kali Yuga, there is disregard for varnashrama dharma—the Shudras and Untouchables wrest power—and chaos reigns, leading to complete destruction. About Kali Yuga, the *Bhagvad Gita* says (IX: 32): "Even those who are of evil birth, women, Vaishyas and Shudras, having sought refuge in me will attain supreme liberation" (Debroy 2005, 137).

Bibliography

Adams, Jad. 2011. *Gandhi: Naked Ambition*. London: Quercus.

Alexander, Michelle. 2010. *The New Jim Crow: Mass Incarceration in the Age of Colorblindness*. New York: The New Press.

Aloysius, G. 1997. *Nationalism Without a Nation in India*. New Delhi: Oxford University Press.

Ambedkar, B.R. 2003. *Ambedkar: Autobiographical Notes*. Ed. Ravikumar. Pondicherry: Navayana.

———. 1979–2003. *Dr Babasaheb Ambedkar: Writings and Speeches* (BAWS). Volumes 1–17. Mumbai: Education Department, Government of Maharashtra.

———. 1992. "Dr Ambedkar's Speech at Mahad." In *Poisoned Bread: Translations from Modern Marathi Dalit Literature*. Ed. Arjun Dangle. Hyderabad: Orient Longman.

Amin, Shahid. 1998. "Gandhi as Mahatma: Gorakhpur District, Eastern UP, 1921–2." In *Selected Subaltern Studies*. Ed. Ranajit Guha and Gayatri Spivak, 288–348. New Delhi: Oxford University Press.

Anand, S. 2002. "Meenakshipuram Redux." *Outlook*, 21 October. http://www.outlookindia.com/article.aspx?217605. Accessed 1 August 2013.

———. 2008a. "Despite Parliamentary Democracy." *Himal*, August. http://www.himalmag.com/component/content/article/838-despite-parliamentary-democracy.html. Accessed 20 July 2013.

———. 2008b. "Understanding the Khairlanji Verdict." *The Hindu*, 5 October.

———. 2009. "Resurrecting the Radical Ambedkar." *Seminar*, September.

———. 2012a. "Between Red And Blue." 16 April. http://www.outlookindia.com/article.aspx?280573. Accessed 10 August 2013.

———. 2012b. "A Case for Bhim Rajya." *Outlook*, 20 August.

Anderson, Perry. 2012. *The Indian Ideology*. New Delhi: Three Essays Collective.

Banerji, Rita. 2008. *Sex and Power: Defining History, Shaping Societies*. New Delhi: Penguin.

———. 2013. "Gandhi used His Position to Sexually Exploit Young Women." 15

October. http://www.youthkiawaaz.com/2013/10/gandhi-used-power
-position-exploit-young-women-way-react-matters-even-today/.
Accessed 20 October 2013.

Bayly, Susan. 1998. "Hindu Modernisers and the 'Public' Arena.
Indigenous Critiques of Caste in Colonial India." In *Vivekananda
and the Modernisation of Hinduism*. Ed. William Radice, 93–137. New
Delhi: Oxford University Press.

Béteille, André. 2001. "Race and Caste." *The Hindu*, 10 March.

Bhasin, Agrima. 2013. "The Railways in Denial." Infochange News and
Features,February.http://infochangeindia.org/human-rights/struggle
-for-human-dignity/the-railways-in-denial.html. Accessed 5 August
2013.

Birla, G.D. 1953. *In the Shadow of the Mahatma: A Personal Memoir*. Calcutta:
Orient Longman.

Breman, Jan. 2004. *The Making and Unmaking of an Industrial Working
Class: Sliding Down the Labour Hierarchy in Ahmedabad, India*. New
Delhi: Oxford University Press.

Buckwalter, Sabrina. 2006. "Just Another Rape Story." *Sunday Times of
India*, 29 October.

Carnegie, Andrew. 1889. *The Gospel of Wealth*. http://www.swarthmore.edu
/SocSci/rbannis1/AIH19th/Carnegie.html. Accessed 26 August 2013.

Chandavarkar, Rajnarayan. 2009. *History, Culture and the Indian City:
Essays*. Cambridge: Cambridge University Press.

Chandra, Uday. 2013. "Liberalism and Its Other: The Politics of
Primitivism in Colonial and Postcolonial Indian Law." *Law & Society
Review* 47 (1): 135–68.

Chawla, Prabhu. 1999. "Courting Controversy." *India Today*, 29 January.

Chitre, Dilip. 2003. *Says Tuka: Selected Poems of Tukaram*. Pune: Sontheimer
Cultural Association.

Chowdhry, Prem. 2007. *Contentious Marriages, Eloping Couples: Gender, Caste
and Patriarchy in Northern India*. New Delhi: Oxford University Press.

Chugtai, Ismat. 2003. *A Chugtai Collection*. Tr. Tahira Naqvi and Syeda S.
Hameed. New Delhi: Women Unlimited.

Damodaran, Harish. 2008. *India's New Capitalists: Caste, Business, and
Industry in a Modern Nation*. New Delhi: Permanent Black.

Dangle, Arjun, ed. 1992. *Poisoned Bread: Translations from Modern Marathi
Dalit Literature*. Hyderabad: Orient Longman.

Das, Bhagwan, ed., 1980. *Rare Prefaces* [of B.R. Ambedkar]. Jullundur:
Bheem Patrika.

———. 2000. "Moments in a History of Reservations". *Economic & Political
Weekly*, 28 October: 3381–4.

———. 2010. *Thus Spoke Ambedkar, Vol.1: A Stake in the Nation*. New Delhi:
Navayana.

Davis, Mike. 2002. *The Great Victorian Holocausts: El Nino Famines and the

Making of the Third World. New York: Verso.

Debroy, Bibek, tr. 2005. *The Bhagavad Gita*. New Delhi: Penguin.

Desai, Ashwin and Goolam Vahed. 2010. *Inside Indian Indenture: A South African Story, 1860–1914*. Cape Town: HSRC Press.

Deshpande, G.P., ed. 2002. *Selected Writings of Jotirao Phule*. New Delhi: LeftWord.

Devji, Faisal. 2012. *The Impossible Indian: Gandhi and the Temptation of Violence*. Cambridge, Massachusetts: Harvard University Press.

Dogra, Chander Suta. 2013. *Manoj and Babli: A Hate Story*. New Delhi: Penguin.

Doniger, Wendy. 2005. *The Rig Veda*. New Delhi: Penguin.

———. and Brian K. Smith. Tr. 1991. *The Laws of Manu*. New Delhi: Penguin Books.

Fischer, Louis. 1951. *The Life of Mahatma Gandhi*. New Delhi: HarperCollins. (Rpr. 1997.)

Gajvee, Premanand. 2013. "Gandhi–Ambedkar." In *The Strength of Our Wrists: Three Plays*. Tr. from Marathi by Shanta Gokhale and M.D. Hatkanangalekar, 91–150. New Delhi: Navayana.

Gandhi, Leela. 1996–97. "Concerning Violence: The Limits and Circulations of Gandhian Ahimsa or Passive Resistance." *Cultural Critique*, 35. 105–47.

Gandhi, Lingaraja. 2004. "Mulk Raj Anand: Quest for So Many Freedoms." *Deccan Herald*, 3 October. http://archive.deccanherald.com /deccanherald/oct032004/sh1.asp. Accessed 5 October 2013.

Gandhi, M.K. 1999. *The Collected Works of Mahatma Gandhi* (Electronic Book). 98 volumes. New Delhi: Publications Division, Government of India.

Ghosh, Suniti Kumar. 2007. *India and the Raj, 1919–1947: Glory, Shame, and Bondage*. Calcutta: Sahitya Samsad.

Godse, Nathuram. 1998. *Why I Assassinated Mahatma Gandhi*. New Delhi: Surya Bharti Prakashan.

Golwalkar, M.S. 1945. *We, or Our Nationhood Defined*. Nagpur: Bharat Prakashan. Fourth ed.

Guha, Ramachandra. 2013a. "What Hindus Can and Should be Proud Of." *The Hindu*, 23 July. http://www.thehindu.com/opinion/lead/what-hindus -can-and-should-be-proud-of/article4941930.ece. Accessed 24 July 2013.

———. 2013b. *India Before Gandhi*. New Delhi: Penguin.

Gupta, Dipankar. 2001. "Caste, Race and Politics." *Seminar*, December.

———. 2007. "Why Caste Discrimination is not Racial Discrimination." *Seminar*, April.

Guru, Gopal. 2012. "Rise of the 'Dalit Millionaire': A Low Intensity Spectacle." *Economic & Political Weekly*, 15 December: 41–49.

Guy, Jeff. 1994. *The Destruction of the Zulu Kingdom: The Civil War in Zululand, 1879–1884*. Pietermaritzburg: University of Natal Press.

———. 2005. *The Maphumulo Uprising: War, Law and Ritual in the Zulu Rebellion*. Scotsville, South Africa: University of KwaZulu-Natal Press.

Hardiman, David. 1996. *Feeding the Baniya: Peasants and Usurers in Western India*. New Delhi: Oxford University Press.

———. 2006. "A Forgotten Massacre: Motilal Tejawat and His Movement amongst the Bhils, 1921–2." In *Histories for the Subordinated*, 29–56. Calcutta: Seagull.

———. 2004. *Gandhi: In His Time and Ours: The Global Legacy of His Ideas*. New York: Columbia University Press.

Hickok, Elonnai. 2012. "Rethinking DNA Profiling in India." *Economic & Political Weekly*, 27 October. Web exclusive piece: http://www.epw.in/web-exclusives/rethinking-dna-profiling-india.html#sdfootnote20anc. Accessed 10 September 2013.

Hochschild, Adam. 2011. *To End All Wars: A Story of Loyalty and Rebellion, 1914–1918*. London: Houghton Mifflin Harcourt.

Human Rights Watch. 1999. *Broken People: Caste Violence against India's "Untouchables"*. New York: Human Rights Watch.

Hutton, J.H. 1935. *Census of India 1931*. Delhi: Government of India.

Ilaiah, Kancha. 1996. *Why I Am Not a Hindu: A Sudra Critique of Hindutva Philosophy, Culture and Political Economy*. Calcutta: Samya.

Jaffrelot, Christophe. 2005. *Dr Ambedkar and Untouchability: Analysing and Fighting Caste*. New Delhi: Permanent Black.

Jamnadas, K. 2010. "*Manusmriti* Dahan Din" [*Manusmriti* burning day]. 14 July. *Round Table India* (roundtableindia.co.in). Accessed 6 September 2013.

Janyala, Sreenivas. 2005. "Tsunami Can't Wash this Away: Hatred for Dalits." *The Indian Express*, 7 January.

Jaoul, Nicolas. 2006. "Learning the Use of Symbolic Means: Dalits, Ambedkar Statues and the State in Uttar Pradesh." *Contributions to Indian Sociology* 40 (2): 175–207.

Jondhale, Surendra and Johannes Beltz. 2004. *Reconstructing the World: B.R. Ambedkar and Buddhism in India*. New Delhi: Oxford University Press.

Joseph, George Gheverghese. 2003. *George Joseph: The Life and Times of a Kerala Christian Nationalist*. Hyderabad: Orient Longman.

Jose, Vinod K. 2010. "Counting Castes." *Caravan*, June.

Josh, Sohan Singh. 2007. *Hindustan Gadar Party: A Short History*. Jalandhar: Desh Bhagat Yadgar Committee. (Orig. publ. 1977.)

Juergensmeyer, Mark. 2009. *Religious Rebels in the Punjab: The Ad Dharm Challenge to Caste*. New Delhi: Navayana. (Orig. publ. 1982.)

Kael, Pauline. 1982. "Tootsie, Gandhi, and Sophie." *The New Yorker*, 27 December.

Kandasamy, Meena. 2013. "How Real-Life Tamil Love Stories End." *Outlook*, 22 July.

Kapur, Devesh, Chandra Bhan Prasad, Lant Pritchett and D. Shyam Babu. 2010. "Rethinking Inequality: Dalits in Uttar Pradesh in the Market

Reform Era." *Economic & Political Weekly.* 28 August: 39–49.

Keer, Dhananjay. 1990. *Dr Ambedkar: Life and Mission.* Mumbai: Popular Prakashan. (Orig. publ. 1954.)

Khandekar, Milind. 2013. *Dalit Millionaires: 15 Inspiring Stories.* Tr. from Hindi by Vandana R. Singh and Reenu Talwar. New Delhi: Penguin.

Kishwar, Madhu. 2006. "Caste System: Society's Bold Mould." *Tehelka*, 11 February http://archive.tehelka.com/story_main16.asp?filename =In021106Societys_12.asp. Accessed 10 October 2013.

Kosambi, D.D. 1948. "Marxism and Ancient Indian Culture." *Annals of the Bhandarkar Oriental Research Institute.* Vol. 26, 271–7.

Krishna, Raj. 1979. "The Nehru Gandhi Polarity and Economic Policy." Ed. B.R. Nanda, P.C. Joshi and Raj Krishna, 51–64. In *Gandhi and Nehru.* New Delhi: Oxford University Press.

Kumar, Vinoj P.C. 2009. "Bringing Out the Dead." *Tehelka*, 4 July. http:// www.tehelka.com/bringing-out-the-dead/#. Accessed 10 August 2013.

———. 2009b. "Numbness of Death." *Tehelka*, 4 July. http://www.tehelka. com/numbness-of-death/. Accessed 10 August 2013.

Lal, Vinay. 2008. "The Gandhi Everyone Loves to Hate." *Economic & Political Weekly*, 4 October: 55–64.

Lelyveld, Joseph. 2011. *Great Soul: Mahatma Gandhi and His Struggle With India.* New York: Alfred A. Knopf.

Mani, Braj Ranjan. 2005. *Debrahmanising History: Dominance and Resistance in Indian Society.* New Delhi: Manohar.

———. 2012. "Amartya Sen's Imagined India." 4 June. http://www .countercurrents.org/mani040612.htm. Accessed 15 July 2013.

Mendelsohn, Oliver and Marika Vicziany. 1998. *The Untouchables: Subordination, Poverty and the State in Modern India.* Cambridge: Cambridge University Press.

Menon, Dilip. 2006. *The Blindness of Insight: Essays on Caste in Modern India.* Pondicherry: Navayana.

Menon, Meena and Neera Adarkar. 2005. *One Hundred Years, One Hundred Voices: The Millworkers of Girangaon: An Oral History.* Calcutta: Seagull.

Menon, Visalakshi. 2003. *From Movement to Government: The Congress in the United Provinces, 1937–42.* New Delhi: Sage.

Mishra, Sheokesh. 2007. "Holy Word." *India Today*, 20 December. http:// indiatoday.intoday.in/story/Holy+word/1/2736.html. Accessed 26 August 2013.

Mohanty, B.B. 2001. "Land Distribution among Scheduled Castes and Tribes." *Economic & Political Weekly*, 6 October: 1357–68.

Mukherjee, Aditya, Mridula Mukherjee and Sucheta Mahajan. 2008. *RSS School Texts and the Murder of Mahatma Gandhi: The Hindu Communal Project.* New Delhi: Sage.

Muktabai (Salve). 1855/1991. "Mang Maharachya Dukhavisayi." Tr. Maya Pandit, "About the Griefs of the Mangs and Mahars." In *Women Writing in India: 600 B.C. to the Present.* Ed. Susie Tharu and K. Lalita,

214–16. New Delhi: Oxford University Press.

Murthy, Srinivasa. 1987. *Mahatma Gandhi and Leo Tolstoy: Letters.* Long Beach: Long Beach Publications.

Nagaraj. D.R. 2010. *The Flaming Feet and Other Essays: The Dalit Movement in India.* Ranikhet: Permanent Black.

Nambissan, Geetha B. 2002. "Equality in Education: The Schooling of Dalit Children in India." In *Dalits and the State.* Ed. Ghanshyam Shah, 79–128. New Delhi: Concept.

Namboodiripad, E.M.S. 1986. *History of the Indian Freedom Struggle.* Trivandrum: Social Scientist Press.

Nandy, Ashis. 1983. *Intimate Enemy: Loss and Recovery of Self under Colonialism.* New Delhi: Oxford University Press.

Natarajan, Balmurli. 2007. "Misrepresenting Caste and Race." *Seminar,* April.

———. and Paul Greenough, ed. 2009. *Against Stigma: Studies in Caste, Race and Justice Since Durban.* Hyderabad: Orient Blackswan.

National Commission for Scheduled Castes and Scheduled Tribes. 1998. *Fourth Report.* New Delhi: NCSCST.

National Crime Records Bureau. 2012. *Crime in India 2011: Statistics.* New Delhi: NCRB, Ministry of Home Affairs.

Nauriya, Anil. 2006. "Gandhi's Little-Known Critique of Varna." *Economic & Political Weekly,* 13 May: 1835–8.

Navaria, Ajay. 2013. *Unclaimed Terrain.* Tr. Laura Brueck. New Delhi: Navayana.

Navsarjan Trust and Robert F. Kennedy Center for Justice & Human Rights. N.d. *Understanding Untouchability: A Comprehensive Study of Practices and Conditions in 1589 Villages.* http://navsarjan.org/Documents/Untouchability_Report_FINAL_Complete.pdf. Accessed 12 September 2013.

Omvedt, Gail. 1994. *Dalits and the Democratic Revolution: Dr Ambedkar and the Dalit Movement in Colonial India.* New Delhi: Sage.

———. 2003. *Buddhism in India: Challenging Brahmanism and Caste.* New Delhi: Sage.

———. 2004. *Ambedkar: Towards an Enlightened India.* New Delhi: Penguin.

———. 2008. *Seeking Begumpura: The Social Vision of Anticaste Intellectuals.* New Delhi: Navayana.

Parel, Anthony, ed. 1997. *'Hind Swaraj' and Other Writings.* Cambridge: Cambridge University Press.

Patel, Sujata. 1988. "Construction and Reconstruction of Women in Gandhi." *Economic & Political Weekly,* 20 February: 377–87.

Patwardhan, Anand. 2011. *Jai Bhim Comrade.* DVD, documentary film.

Phadke, Y.D. 1993. *Senapati Bapat: Portrait of a Revolutionary.* New Delhi: National Book Trust.

Prashad, Vijay. 1996. "The Untouchable Question." *Economic & Political Weekly,* 2 March: 551–9.

———. 2001. *Untouchable Freedom: A Social History of a Dalit Community*. New Delhi: Oxford University Press.

Pyarelal. 1932. *The Epic Fast*. Ahmedabad: Navajivan.

Raman, Anuradha. 2010. "Standard Deviation." *Outlook*, 26 April.

Ramaswamy, Gita. 2005. *India Stinking: Manual Scavengers in Andhra Pradesh and Their Work*. Chennai: Navayana.

Ravikumar. 2009. *Venomous Touch: Notes on Caste, Culture and Politics*. Calcutta: Samya.

Rege, Sharmila. 2013. *Against the Madness of Manu: B.R. Ambedkar's Writings on Brahmanical Patriarchy*. New Delhi: Navayana.

Renold, Leah. 1994. "Gandhi: Patron Saint of the Industrialist." *Sagar: South Asia Graduate Research Journal* 1 (1): 16–38.

Sainath, P. 2013a. "Over 2,000 Fewer Farmers Every Day." *The Hindu*, 2 May.

———. 2013b. "Farmers' Suicide Rates Soar Above the Rest." *The Hindu*, 18 May.

———. 1999a. "One People, Many Identities." *The Hindu*, 31 January.

———. 1999b. "After Meenakshipuram: Caste, Not Cash, Led to Conversions." *The Hindu*, 7 February.

Santhosh S. and Joshil K. Abraham. 2010. "Caste Injustice in Jawaharlal Nehru University." *Economic & Political Weekly*, 26 June: 27–9.

Satyanarayana, K. and Susie Tharu, ed. 2013. *The Exercise of Freedom: An Introduction to Dalit Writing*. New Delhi: Navayana.

Savarkar, V.D. 1923. *Hindutva*. Nagpur: V.V. Kelkar.

Sen, Dwaipayan. 2010. "A Politics Subsumed." *Himal*, April.

Singh, G.B. 2004. *Gandhi: Behind the Mask of Divinity*. New York: Prometheus Books.

Singh, Khushwant. 1990. "Brahmin Power." *Sunday*, 29 December.

Singh, Patwant. 1999. *The Sikhs*. London: John Murray/New Delhi: Rupa.

Skaria, Ajay. 2006. "Only One Word, Properly Altered: Gandhi and the Question of the Prostitute." *Economic & Political Weekly*, 9 December: 5065–72.

Swan, Maureen. 1984. "The 1913 Natal Indian Strike." *Journal of Southern African Studies* 10 (2): 239–58.

———. 1985. *Gandhi: The South African Experience*. Johannesburg: Ravan Press.

Tagore, Rabindranath. 2007. *The English Writings of Rabindranath Tagore, Vol 2: Poems*. New Delhi: Atlantic.

Teltumbde, Anand. 2005. *Anti-Imperialism and Annihilation of Castes*. Thane: Ramai Prakashan.

———. 2010a. *The Persistence of Caste: The Khairlanji Murders and India's Hidden Apartheid*. New Delhi: Navayana/London: Zed Books.

———. 2010b. "Dangerous Sedative". *Himal*, April. http://www.himalmag .com/component/content/article/132-.html. Accessed 20 August 2013.

———. 2012. "It's Not Red vs. Blue." *Outlook*, 20 August. http://www

.outlookindia.com/article.aspx?281944. Accessed 22 August 2013.
——— and Shoma Sen, ed. 2012a. *Scripting the Change: Selected Writings of Anuradha Ghandy*. New Delhi: Danish Books.
———. 2013. "*Aerocasteics* of Rahul Gandhi." *Economic & Political Weekly*: 2 November: 10–11.
Tharu, Susie and K. Lalita, ed. 1997. *Women Writing in India, Vol. 1: 600 B.C. to the Early Twentieth Century*. New Delhi: Oxford University Press. (Orig. publ. 1991.)
Thorat, S.K. and Umakant, ed. 2004. *Caste, Race, and Discrimination: Discourses in International Context*. New Delhi: Rawat.
———. 2009. *Dalits in India: Search for a Common Destiny*. New Delhi: Sage.
Tidrick, Kathryn. 2006. *Gandhi: A Political and Spiritual Life*. London: I.B. Tauris.
Valmiki, Omprakash. 2003. *Joothan: A Dalit's Life*. Calcutta: Samya.
Vanita, Ruth. 2002. "Whatever Happened to the Hindu Left?" *Seminar*, April.
Viswanathan, S. 2005. *Dalits in Dravidian Land: Frontline Reports on Anti-Dalit Violence in Tamil Nadu (1995–2004)*. Chennai: Navayana.
Viswanath, Rupa. 2012. "A Textbook Case of Exclusion." *The Indian Express*, 20 July.
———. 2014 (forthcoming). *The Pariah Problem: Caste, Religion, and the Social in Modern India*. New York: Columbia University Press/New Delhi: Navayana.
Vyam, Durgabai, Subhash Vyam, Srividya Natarajan and S. Anand. 2011. *Bhimayana: Experiences of Untouchability*. New Delhi: Navayana.
Weiss, Gordon. 2011. *The Cage: The Fight for Sri Lanka and the Last Days of the Tamil Tigers*. London: The Bodley Head.
Wolpert, Stanley. 1993. *A New History of India*. New York: Oxford University Press. (Orig. Publ. 1973.)
Zelliot, Eleanor. 2013. *Ambedkar's World: The Making of Babasaheb and the Dalit Movement*. New Delhi: Navayana.
Zinn, Howard and Anthony Arnove. 2004. *Voices of a People's History of the United States*. New York: Seven Stories Press.

Index

fear of saliva. *See* saliva, fear of
First World War. *See* World War I
Fischer, Louis, 111, 137–38n165
forced eating of excrement, 5,
    126–27n9

Gaekwad, Sayajirao, 80
Gandhi (Attenborough), 23
Gandhi, Devdas, 73, 139n195
Gandi, Lingaraja, 138–39n187
Gandhi, Mohandas, vii, viii,
    32–34 passim, 42–81 passim;
    Ambedkar relations, 21, 22–
    23, 27, 48, 77, 104, 108–10,
    140n201; Anglo-Boer war,
    52–55 passim; assassination,
    47–48, 112; Baloo and,
    144n244; Bambatha
    Rebellion, 55–56; biographies,
    49, 68, 72, 75, 111; on cows,
    144–43n246; eating, 58, 61,
    62, 86, 136n136, 139n194;
    Hind Swaraj, 65–68, 137n155;
    hunger strike, 108–9, 110,
    114; inconsistency, 49,
    55–61 passim; 'Indo-Aryan'
    belief, 51; jail/prison time,
    57–58, 108, 110; Kaisar-i-
    Hind Medal, 72; Khilifat
    movement, 44, 45, 88;
    Mahad Satyagraha, 93;
    'Mahatmahood', 48–49,
    68, 72–77 passim; miracles
    alleged, 76; Mussolini
    meetings, 45, 108; partition
    of Pakistan, 46–47; patrons/
    sponsors, 61, 72–73, 90,
    96, 137–38n165; Phoenix
    Settlement, 56; purity
    and renunciation, 49,
    61–62, 63; revisionism,
    72; Salt Satyagraha, 106,
    107; 'Sanatani Hindu', 43;
    Satyagraha in South Africa,

55–56; on satyagraha vs.
    duragraha, 93, 140n206;
    sexuality and celibacy, 26,
    56, 61–62, 63, 131n59; South
    Africa, 49–62 passim; Temple
    Entry Bill, 114; thirst for
    money, 90; Tolstoy Farm,
    61, 62, 63–64; valorisation
    of villages, 32–33, 67–68,
    101; vegetarianism, 61; view
    of industrialism, 33; view
    of resistance against dam-
    building, 133n76; views
    of black Africans, 51, 56,
    57–58, 67–69 passim, 76,
    101, 118; views of capitalism
    and wealth, 62–63, 74–75,
    96–97, 124; views of caste and
    inequality, viii, 9–10, 25–26,
    62, 68, 74–75; views of Dalits/
    Untouchability, 61, 85–86,
    89, 104, 108–18 passim, 138–
    39n187; views of poverty, 56,
    62; views of scavengers and
    latrine cleaners, 85, 116–17,
    139n188; views of women and
    girls, 63–65; views of working
    class and strikes, 96–97
Gandhi, Rahul, 24, 139n189
Germany, 46, 53, 136n121
Ghadar Party, 41, 135n95
Girni Kamgar Union, 94
girls. *See* women and girls
Godhra train-coach burning,
    2002, 120
Godse, Nathuram, 47–48, 112
Goenka family, 16
Gokhale, Gopal Krishna, 78
Goldman, Emma, 59
Golwalkar, M.S., 46
The Gospel of Wealth (Carnegie), 75
Goswami, Rajiv, 143n230
government employment. *See* civil
    service employment

Muslim League, 24, 46, 119, 122

Muslims, 15, 28, 37–45 passim,
61, 66, 87–91 passim, 134n84;
abuse of Untouchables, 115;
Ambedkar and, 81; Congress
party and, 44; Pakistan,
47; pogroms against, 120;
'political Islam', 119; Sachar
Committee, 140n33; in
Scheduled Castes definition,
126n6; separate electorate, 42,
80, 108

Mussolini, Benito, 45, 46, 108

Naicker, E.V. Ramasamy, 22

Namboodiripad, E.M.S., 99

Narayana Guru, 22

Narayanan, K.R., 17–18

Natal Indian Congress, 50–51, 53

nationalisation, 122

Naxalites, 100, 103

Nehru, Jawaharlal, 47, 58, 109,
146–47n275

A New History of India (Wolpert), 46

The New Jim Crow (Alexander),
111

newspapers. *See* press

Non-Cooperation Movement,
44–45, 72

nongovernmental organisations
(NGOs), 73, 101, 141n221

opinion polls, 23, 131n53

Ottoman Empire, 44

Pakistan, 2, 24, 37, 122; partition,
46–47, 119

Pandharpur, 32, 34

Paraiyans, 1, 5

Parsis, 12, 66, 81

'passenger Indians'. *See* South
Africa

Pass Laws (South Africa), 60, 69

Patels, 120

patriarchy, 59, 64–65

peasant movement. *See* kisan
(peasant) movement

Peshwas, 78

Phule, Jotiba, 21, 37, 60, 78, 100,
115, 119; *Gulamgiri*, 66

pogroms, anti-Muslim, 120

Polak, Henry, S.L., 70; *M.K.
Gandhi*, 68

polls. *See* opinion polls

'pollution-purity matrix', 7, 44, 82

Poona Pact, 110–15 passim, 121

Pouchepadass, Jacques, 73–74

poverty, 20, 56, 62, 67, 74, 92,
128n24; of Ambedkar, 123

Prabuddha Bharat, 32

Prasad, Rajendra, 30

Prashad, Vijay, 86

Premnagar, 32, 34

press, 15–16, 54, 56, 70, 73, 88,
91; Ambedkar-founded, 32,
140n202; Dalit, 22; Gandhi-
founded, 113; on M. Gandhi,
76

Prevention of Atrocities Act.
See Scheduled Castes and
Scheduled Tribes Prevention
of Atrocities Act

privatisation, 19, 129n35

protests: against atrocities, 3,
126n7; against British
government, 99; against
dams, 133n76; against job
quotas, 18, 19, 142–43n230;
against M. Gandhi, 52;
against Rowlatt Act, 44;
against South African Pass
Laws, 60. *See also* Champaran
Satyagraha; Mahad
Satyagraha; Salt Satyagraha;
satyagraha and duragraha;
Vaikom Satyagraha

public employment. *See* civil
service employment

Arundhati Roy studied architecture in Delhi, where she now lives. She is the author of the novel *The God of Small Things*, for which she received the 1997 Booker Prize. The novel has been translated into more than forty languages worldwide. She has written several nonfiction books, including *Field Notes on Democracy: Listening to Grasshoppers*, *Capitalism: A Ghost Story*, *Walking with the Comrades*, *Things That Can and Cannot Be Said* (with John Cusack), and *The End of Imagination*. She is the recipient of the 2002 Lannan Cultural Freedom Prize, the 2015 Ambedkar Sudar award, and the 2015 Mahatma Jyotiba Phule Award from the Mahatma Phule Samata Parishad.

About Haymarket Books

Haymarket Books is a nonprofit, progressive book distributor and publisher, a project of the Center for Economic Research and Social Change. We believe that activists need to take ideas, history, and politics into the many struggles for social justice today. Learning the lessons of past victories, as well as defeats, can arm a new generation of fighters for a better world. As Karl Marx said, "The philosophers have merely interpreted the world; the point, however, is to change it."

We take inspiration and courage from our namesakes, the Haymarket Martyrs, who gave their lives fighting for a better world. Their 1886 struggle for the eight-hour day reminds workers around the world that ordinary people can organize and struggle for their own liberation.

For more information and to shop our complete catalog of titles, visit us online at www.haymarketbooks.org.

Also Available from Haymarket Books
by Arundhati Roy

The End of Imagination

Things That Can and Cannot Be Said: Essays and Conversations
John Cusack and Arundhati Roy

Field Notes on Democracy: Listening to Grasshoppers

Capitalism: A Ghost Story

9 781608 467976